AF559894

SOCIO-ECONOMIC CONDITIONS OF SELF-EMPLOYED WORKERS

SOCIO-ECONOMIC CONDITIONS OF SELF-EMPLOYED WORKERS

By

Dr. T. Jeyanthi Vijayarani

M. Com, Ph.D.

Associate Professor

Department of Commerce

Fatima College, Madurai-625 018

Tamil Nadu

(India)

DISCOVERY PUBLISHING HOUSE PVT. LTD.

NEW DELHI-110 002

Published by:
Tilak Wasan
DISCOVERY PUBLISHING HOUSE PVT. LTD.
4831/24, Prahlad Street, Ansari Road
Darya Ganj, New Delhi-110002 (India)
Phone: +91-11-23279245, 43764432
Fax: +91-11-23253475
E-mail: parul.wasan@gmail.com
discoverypublishinghouse@gmail.com
info@discoverypublishinggroup.com
web: www.discoverypublishinggroup.com

***First Edition:* 2011**
ISBN: 978-81-8356-921-7

Socio-economic Conditions of Self-employed Workers

Printed at:
Shree Balaji Art Press
Delhi

Preface

I praise Almighty Lord Jesus Christ for his showers of blessing on me for the successful outcome of this book. Thy grace has helped me to publish this book.

In developing countries, self-employment is mostly necessity. An attempt to start their own business brings them a better position than they were before. Self-employment is the work done by a person by running a business on behalf of their own expense and at their own risk. Self-employed worker is an independent worker who works independently of an employer. Self-employed earn livelihood from their trade or business rather than as an employee of another and uses a hands on approach to survive. Terms such as self-employed, entrepreneurs and business owners are interchangeable and functionally speaking all entre-preneurs are self-employed and encompasses artisans covering potters, weavers, basket makers, metalworkers, *beedi* workers, *agarbathi* workers, *papad* rollers, vendors etc.

Many of the policy-makers consider self-employment as an attainable solution to the crisis in employment. The wave of entrepreneurs raised with experience enables them to become successful in their métier. Self-employed find livelihood for them and are able to stem up the socio-economic condition. Socio arrive from social and speak of social conditions such as age, sex, family size, marriage and divorce. The word 'economic' specifies the economic conditions such as income, savings, expenditure, occupational status etc.

This book on *'Socio-Economic Conditions of Self-employed Workers'* is an outcome of a research study undertaken by me with the broad objective of analysing the present status of potters and women entrepreneurs, their living and working conditions and the major problems and challenges met by them. It is my earnest hope that this book will provide sufficient use to the students, researches, academicians, policymakers, government and non-governmental organisations.

Dr. T. Jeyanthi Vijayarani

Acknowledgements

I wish to place on record my heartfelt thanks and gratitude to the respectable and honourable distinguished professor Dr. Punithavathy Pandian, Department of Commerce, Madurai Kamaraj University for her encouragement and all time support and prayers to publish this book.

I sincerely thank the management Rev. Sr. Esther Mary, Secretary, Rev. Dr. Sr. Jospin Nirmala Mary, Principal, and Rev. Dr. Sr. P.A. Mary Vice Principal, Fatima College, Madurai for their kind encouragement and support to publish this book.

I thank all my colleagues in the Department of Commerce and all my friends for the interest shown by them to bring out this book.

My sincere gratitude to my beloved mother Mrs. Jeevarathnam, my brother, sisters and in-laws for their honest support. My husband Mr. T. Jason Premkumar and my daughter J. Jashny Prettina who upholded me with prayer to bring out this book.

I will be failing my duty if I do not acknowledge the help rendered by SIPPO, CAPART, NGO's, Chamber of Commerce, DIC and KVIC. I'm especially thankful to the selected potters and women entrepreneurs for their co-operation, opinion and suggestions.

On behalf of all the contributors, friends and family members I am obliged to thank Mr. Tilak Wasan, Proprietor, M/s. Discovery Publishing House Pvt Ltd, New Delhi for his consent to publish this book.

Dr. T. Jeyanthi Vijayarani

Contents

A Study on Socio-economic Conditions of Women Entrepreneurs

Abbreviations

BPL	—	Below Poverty Line
CAPART	—	Council for Advancement of People Action and Rural Technology
DIC	—	District Industries Centres
IRDP	—	Intergrated Rural Development Programe
KAWTF	—	Khadi Artisans Welfare Trust Fund
KVIB	—	Khadi Village and Industries Board
KVIC	—	Khadi Village and Industries Commission
NABARD	—	National Bank for Agricultural and Rural Development
NGOs	—	Non-Governmental Organizations
SIPPO	—	Small Industries Products Promotion Organisation
SSI	—	Small Scale Industries
TRYSEM	—	Training and Rural Youth for Self Employment
VI	—	Village Industries

A STUDY ON SOCIO-ECONOMIC CONDITIONS OF RURAL ARTISANS

—Dr. T. Jeyanthi Vijayarani & M. Ananthi

CHAPTER

Introduction and Design of the Study

Introduction

Potters must have been the first tribe of artisans that existed in India. The origin of pottery in India can be traced back to the Neolithic age. Harrapan and Mohanjodaro cultures heralded the age of wheel-made pottery. The phase of glazed pottery started in the 12th century AD, when Muslim rulers encouraged potters from the Middle East to settle in India. Glazed pottery of Persian models with Indian designs, dating back to the sultanate period has been found in Gujarat. The first pottery unit run in India was by Sir S Deb, in Calcutta. It established the success of high-class pottery made out of clay. Porcelain factories were set up in Gwalior and Calcutta in the first decade of 20th century.[1] Today, the pottery is run on both cottage and modern lines. Hundreds of small and big factories all over the country keep this age-old tradition alive. In Indian villages, around 15 lakhs potters with traditional skill are playing their profession. About 95 per cent of them are engaged in the traditional red or local clay pottery work. The extent of employment of outsiders in the village pottery activities is about 9 per cent. The rest 91 per cent are potters family members who assist the potters in various operations, from preparation of clay to baking the raw products in the kiln.

Technology that came from time to time has introduced a whole range of vessels and household utensils that pottery is gradually being marginalized from the mainstream utility items at the household level even in many of the villages. That a class of artisans being is marginalized goes without saying and that a section of the population is being left without the livelihood opportunity that they depended on for years. In Tamil Nadu State that there are 50,585 potters in Tamil Nadu. Making glazed pottery items using china clay was successful with the support of the Khadi and Village Industries Commission (KVIC). After Khadi and Village Industries Commission minimized its support , the unit is facing severe financial crisis and it is not able to meet the working capital requirement to procure raw materials such as china clay, chemicals, stone-materials, firewood etc. The profit earned by the potters also has declined as the cost of production has increased.

Potters are not completely blind to market trends as one thinks. Apart from producing glazed pottery and terracotta items, potters also are involved in innovation to remain in the market. They make certain items which attract the attention when one passes by in an exhibition like Magic lamp - a kerosene –light lamp etc. The Khadi and Village Industries Commission and United Nations Development Programme (UNDP) have helped introduce a whole range of improved tools, machineries and technology in pottery.

In typical Tamil Nadu villages pottery articles are gradually becoming less and less as years go by. Stainless and other durable materials have increasingly started occupying the place of pottery articles. The potters are aware of the fact that the market and modernity are marginalization the pottery traditional for ethnic items. Institutional agencies of the government such as the Tamil Nadu Handicrafts Development Corporation, Khadi and Village Industries Commission and the Department of Cooperatives of the government are not in position to support potters through finance and marketing assistances, to the extent required.

Increasing role of fashion, trends and market dynamics keep silently communicating to the potters that they should turn to doing red pottery articles and terracotta items only for the antique shops in five star hotels and not for any use value as it used to be with in ancient kitchens. Pottery requires protection and support. Potters need to identify and cash in on, by propagating the science associated with using pottery articles in addition to communicating the ethnic value it stands for.[2]

Statement of the Problem

Pottery is one of the traditional industries in Tamil Nadu. The rural population earns their livelihood from agriculture and pot making. The availability of land, sources of raw materials, working shed and furnaces is scarce. A limited segment of the society understands that the preservation of water in earthen pots and cooking in earthen pots is safe. Stainless and other durable materials have increasingly started occupying the place of pottery articles. The potters are not able to compete with present market because the traditional techniques are still in practice. The number of people to whom pottery sold is few. All the potters are not aware of the market trends also. Though the Government lends financial assistances to potters through its agencies they are unable to avail these benefits due to their ignorance and unawareness. This drives them to the local money lenders who exploit them.[3]

At present, the financial assistance given by Khadi and Village Industries Commissions is also minimised and the potters are facing severe financial crisis. So, the researcher has made an attempt to analyse the socio-economic condition of potters in Madurai city.

Review of Literature

Mane (1987) examined that only a small percentage of handicraft products are marketed through the public agencies, rest is handled by private traders. Mane highlighted the lack of attention given by the governmental institutions in attending to the essential needs of artisans and craftsmen.[4]

Sreerangi (1987) critically evaluates the policy benefits which accrue to the craftsmen and artisans. He found that all these measures are unsuccessful in controlling the exploitation of the artisans and the craftsmen.[5]

Carla M. Sinopoli (1996) has conducted a research on "Ceramic Use and Ritual Practices in Hindu India" and stated the use of ceramic vessels and figurines in Hindu rituals which has a history that can be traced for more than 2000 years. It was observed that indian potters face threats to their traditional occupation from the increasing availability of low cost plastic and aluminum alternatives to ceramic vessels. Besides, it was concluded that the role of potters and their economic status will undoubtedly change and the future of this ancient craft would be assured by the continued need for ceramic vessels and figurines for the many rituals that are so much a part of daily life in the Hindu world.[6]

The focuses of attention given on (1997) "The Kumbaran of India" are a sub-caste of the Chettiars, which includes all who work with mud or clay (tile makers, brick makers, and potters). Many Kumbaran have become "coolie" workers because of the loss of the traditional markets for their products due to the competition in plastic and aluminum goods. By providing employment and training, upgrading their products to meet export market standards are the remedial measures.[7]

Hari D Goyal (2000) conducted a study on "Impact Assessment Study of Socio-Economic Development Programmes". The objective of the programme is to enable the rural artisans to enhance the quality of the product, increase the production and their income and lead a better quality of life with use of modern tools, since all traditional rural artisans living below the poverty line. Apart from the benefits available under IRDP and TRYSEM, who are trained under TRYSEM are eligible for assistance under the programme.[8]

Radhika Vaidyanathan (2001) in her study "The Velar Makers of Ritual Terracotta" focused on the process of making the large terracotta figures by the potters, as a team work for the village festival. She stated that the Velar community is associated with the rituals performed at village temples who themselves express the idea that they turn natural materials into useful cultural products.[9]

Srijan se shakti (2001) conducted a study on "Chinhat pottery", Lucknow and the survey was aimed to analyse the plight of artisans and marketing potentials for pottery, ceramics and terracotta products. The results suggested a significant opportunities for growth and development of chinhat pottery in Lucknow.[10]

Lalitha Bamba (2002) in her project on "Techno-socio-economic survey of the traditional potter" investigated the status of the potters communities and their working and living conditions. She also examined the scope for improving their productivity through simple mechanisation and value addition to their products.[11]

Vasanth Shinde (2002) in his article "Ethno-Archaeological study of Pottery Manufacture" has made attempt to study the various processes of the pottery manufacturing and need for having different kinds of forms and their functions. He also dealt with the process of the acquisition of raw materials, firing pots in kiln, distribution pattern and the status of potters. It also explains the various features associated with pottery manufacture and how this modern data is useful in understanding the pottery of remote past.[12]

Archana Choksi (2003) in her article, dealt with the "Pottery manufacture in Kutch"and aimed to analyse the traditional techniques used in the manufacture of pottery in the village of Kutch. The tools and techniques that are used by the potters of kutch today which survived for many centuries was stated. It was highlighted that each stage of the vessel making process from the mining of the clay through to the final decoration and distribution of the pots.[13]

The study undertaken by Shailesh Kumar Singh (2005) "Living on the Edge - An Appraisal of Livelihoods in Rural Jharkhand". Artisan is another sector that provides livelihood opportunities to majority of rural poor in the state. The artisanship are primarily based on the existing resources of that particular area such as wood, leaves, minor forest produces, clay, stones. The other interesting fact revealed during the study was to know the seasonality of artisan work and it also explored the enabling and restricting factors for artisans. The enabling factors such as less capital, part time engagement, traditional occupation and restricting factors such as limited market, low income and lack of storage facilities.[14]

Naresh Bhatnagar, (2005) in their study on "Potters wheel development – a necessity for rural growth" has made an attempt to bring out the concept of improvements in potters wheel for carrying out work in different segments and conditions which prevail – smaller or bigger size. It also brings out technology overview towards commercialization and associated and business opportunities. The study concludes that by developing the improvisation in the potters wheel not only increase the production rate but also helps in manpower, energy savings, ease of operation, less time consumption for fabrications and potters can also concentrate in developing more value added products.[15]

Naba Kumar Duray (2007) in his study the "Traditional Hira Potters of Lower Assam", stated that the particular community is strong in their traditional beliefs in pottery work, which is made by the women folk and he aiso examined the present status of crafts and artisans, techniques of pottery production and sale of finished products. It was concluded that the Hira people lives under the shroud poverty and unless appropriate measures are taken this inherent craft will not survive.[16]

The study conducted by Suresh (2007) regarding the "Mitigating Health Risks in the Pottery Sector Caste Study in Kumbharwada, Mumbai", reveals Kumbharwada located in the Dharavi slum of Mumbai is a community of some 1200 families, about half of which are involved in pottery production. It was observed that the Potters relied on cheap fuel such as cotton dust and oil-soaked cotton to fire their brick kilns producing heavy air pollution and contributing to major health problems in the surrounding area with little return. The main aim of the study was to introduce, facilitate and document the social and environmental changes in Kumbharwada by introducing gas kilns to replace the traditional brick ones. He opined that the new technology would significantly reduce emissions, enhance efficiency and make it possible to diversify the product. The study concluded that working and living conditions of potters in kumbharawada are not satisfactory.[17]

Daniel Paul (2007) has examined an "Evaluation study of rural tourism scheme". The prime motive of the rural tourism scheme is to enhance the capacity of local artisans. The various implementing agencies have conducted different workshops, seminars to provide value addition to existing artisan's skills. Hence, an attempt has been made in exposing the arts and crafts of the village generating income to artisans and over all reveal of the rich heritage of the village.[18]

Bula Sirika (2008) in her study on "Socio-economic Status of Handicrafts Women" focused the producers of implements and utensils that many people used in day to day activities. It was observed that the economic status has been adversely affected by technological factors in rural markets. The study concludes that major socio-economic challenges for artisans were identified and appropriate measures also were taken.[19]

Charu Smita Gupta (2008) in her article "Clay-traditional material for making Handicrafts" the main focus of attention to observe that clay and terracotta figures have been existing continuously from pre-historic times. She discussed in her article about the variety of the clay components, shaping and firing techniques used to create variety of forms. The article concluded that, most of the clay items and storage containers have been replaced by metallic containers and on the other hand the earthen pots still used for storing drinking water.[20]

Pyare Lal (2009) made a study of rural artisans working in different trade in his article "Status of Rural Artisan in Bihar. In his analysis, it was clear that factor such as proper training, supply of toolkits, technical and financial assistances were important for the upliftment of artisans.[21]

Parthasarathy in his book titled "The Pattern of production and market for artisan goods" highlighted that the rural artisans face difficult market conditions partly as a result of the declining demand for some of the traditional items produced by the artisans and their limited diversification into production of new items. It was concluded that the artisan workers cope with these conditions by engaging themselves in agriculture and other subsidiary activities.[22]

Sataya Sunadaram in his book titled "Rural Development" highlighted that the artisans can survive in a competitive world only when they possess the capacity to diversify and modernize their skills in tune with present needs. [23]

Scope of the Study

The present study highlights the status of traditional potters as well as their working and living conditions. The study also focuses on the problem faced by potters and tries to identify the remedial measures to improve pottery business.

Objectives of the Study

The objectives of the study are:

- To study the theoretical background of the rural artisans.
- To examine the socio-economic conditions of potters.
- To analyse problems faced by the potters.
- To give suggestions on the basis of findings.

Hypotheses

To give specific focus to the objectives, a few hypotheses have been drawn up and tested using appropriate statistical tools:

- Savings of the potters are not related to age, education and income.
- There is no significant in the ranks assign by different potters regarding the source of savings.
- There is no significant difference between the age and the level of satisfaction of the potters.
- There is no significant relationship between willingness to continue and the level of satisfaction of the potters.

Research Design and Methodology

Research Design

Exploratory research has been used for this study purpose. It is meant to provide more information about the problem or of developing working hypothesis from an operational point of view.

Sampling Technique

The stratified random sampling method is adopted. The potters who are registered with DIC, KVIC, SIPPO, and CAPART are considered as stratas. From each strata, a sample of 30 potters are selected equally from each institution.

Collection of Data

The study includes only primary data. The primary data were collected through well-structured interview schedule from 120 potters in Madurai city.

Framework of Analysis

Factor analysis, Chi-square test, Garret's ranking technique, Weighted average method, Intensity value, One-way ANOVA, Kendall coefficient of concordance, Multiple

Regression, Percentage analysis, bar diagram and pie diagram were used to analyse the data.

Chi-square Test

Chi-square test is a non-parametric test which is used for comparing a sample variance to a theoretical population variance. The chi-square test is applied when the cell frequency is more than 5.

$$\chi^2 = \frac{\Sigma(O-E)^2}{E}$$

O = Observed Frequency
E = Expected Frequency

$$E = \frac{\text{Row total} \times \text{Column total}}{\text{Grand Total}}$$

$\nu = (C-1)\,(r-1)$
ν = Degrees of freedom

Where the calculated value is less than the table value the hypothesis is accepted.

Garret's Ranking Technique

The following formula was used in Garrett's ranking technique.

$$\text{Per cent portion} = \frac{100\,(R_{ij} - 0.5)}{N_{ij}}$$

R_{ij} = Rank given for the ith variables by the jth respondents
N_{ij} = Number of variables ranked by the jth respondent.

By referring to the Garrett's table, the percentage position estimated was converted into scores. Thus, for each factor, the score of various respondents were added and the mean score was estimated. The means thus obtained for each of the attributes were arranged in a descending order. The attributes with the highest mean score was considered as the most important and the factors followed in order.

Weighted Average Method

Weighted Average Method is used to rank the source of borrowing four point rating scale is used and each scale has given a score according to the importance starting from 4 to 1.

$$\text{Weighted Average} = X_w = \frac{\Sigma WX}{\Sigma W}$$

Where $\bar{X} w$ = Weighted Arithmetic mean

W = The weightage attached to variables

X = The variable value.

Intensity Value

To study the reason for continuing pottery work five reasons are framed and for each reason Likert's scaling technique had been used. The scores were given in the order of five, four, three, two and one for Rank 1, 2, 3, 4, and 5 respectively for each reason. The intensity value was calculated as follows:

Intensity value: $[R_1{*}5 + R_2{*}4 + R_3{*}3 + R_4{*}2 + R_5{*}1]$

R = Represents the ranks.

Analysis of Variance Table for one way ANOVA
(There are k samples having in all n items)

Source of variation	Sum of Squares (SS)	Degrees of freedom (d.f)	Mean squares (MS) (This is SS divided by d.f.) and is estimation of variance to be used in F-ratio	F – ratio
Between samples or categories	$n_1 (x1-x)^2 + \ldots + n_k (X_k - x)2$	(k – 1)	$\frac{\text{SS between}}{(k - 1)}$	$\frac{\text{Ms between}}{\text{Ms within}}$
With in samples or categories	$\Sigma(X_{ji} - X_1)^2 + \ldots + S(X_{ki} - X_K)^2$	(n – k)	$\frac{\text{SS within}}{(n - k)}$	
Total	$\Sigma(Xij - X)2$ i = 1,2,.... j = 1,2,....	(n – 1)		

One-Way Anova

Under the one-way ANOVA, only one factor is considered than it is observed that the reason for said factor to be important is that several possible types of samples can occur within that factor. It is then determine if there are differences with in that factor.

Kendall's Coefficient of Concordance

Kendall is a non-parametric measure of relationship. It is used for determining the degree of association among several sets of ranking of *N* objects or individuals.

$$W = \frac{S}{1/12k^2\left(N^3 - N\right)}$$

Where $S = E(Rj - \bar{R}j)^2$

k = No. of sets of ranking

N = Number of objects ranked;

$1/12k^2 (N^3 - N)$= Maximum possible sum of the squared deviations.

Multiple Regression

When there are two or more independent variables, the equation describing relationship as the multiple regression equation, multiple regression taking only two or more independent variables and one dependent variable.

Factor Analysis

Factor analysis is a general name denoting a class of procedures primarily used for data reduction and summarization the factor may be represented as;

$$X_i = A_{i1}F_1 + A_{i2}F_2 + A_{i3}F_3 + \ldots + A_{im}F_m + V_iU_i$$

Where

X_i = ith standardized variable

A_{ij} = standardized mulitple regression coefficient of variable I on common factor i.

E = common factor j

V_i = standardized regression coefficient of variable I on unique factor i.

U_i = the unique factor for variable i

m = number of common factors.

The unique factors are uncorrelated with each other and with the common factors. The common factors themselves can be expressed as linear combinations of the observed variables.

$$F_i = W_{i1}X_1 + W_{i2}X_2 + W_{i3}X_3 + \ldots + W_{ik}X_k$$

Where

F_i = estimate of ith factor.

W_i = weight or factor score coefficient

K = number of variables.

Percentage Analysis

Percentage analysis is a simplest tool used by all. It is used to give the clear cut information about the anlaysis.

$$\text{Percentage} = \frac{\text{Individual respondent}}{\text{Total number of respondent}} \times 100$$

Operational Definitions

Rural Artisans

A person who is engaged in some of the village and cottage industry and derives the major income from that is termed as rural artisans.

The Reserve Bank of India declared certain ingredients to consider a person as an artisan depending upon the profession in which the person is mainly engaged. Occupations make it clear such as Potters, Blacksmith, Goldsmith, Stone carvers, Carpenters, Weavers, Basket makers, Leather workers, Metal workers.[23]

Handicrafts

Handicrafts are mostly defined as Items made by hand, often with the use of simple tools, and are generally artistic and also objects of utility and objects of decoration.[24]

Craftsmen

Somebody who makes decorative or practical objects skilfully by hand.[25]

Tools Kits

Set of tools especially for specific type of work and helps to improve the productivity of rural artisan and reduce the drudgery of work.

Pottery

Pottery termed as object that are first shape of wet clay and then hardened by baking. Pottery includes both decorative under practical items such as Bowls, Vase, Dishes, and Lamps.

Limitations of the study

The term artisan includes the whole array of artisans and potters. But the study includes only potters among those who are conventionally accepted as tradition rural artisans such as goldsmiths, blacksmiths, carpenters, vessel makers and Stone carvers.

Chapter Scheme

The report has been organised and presented in six chapters.

- The introduction, statement of the problem, Review of literature, scope of the study, objectives of the study, hypotheses, methodology, frame work of analysis and the chapter scheme are presented in the first chapter.

- The second chapter deals with the theoretical background of the rural artisans and the potters.
- The socio-economic conditions of the potters are analysed in the third chapter.
- The fourth chapter includes the analysis of the problems faced by the potters.
- The fifth chapter is a summation of findings and suggestions.

REFERENCES

1. Sumati Jeet, *Handicraft year book 1986*, Handicraft industry, p. 413.
2. www. handicraft.indiamart.com
3. Dr. G. Palanidurai, *Decentralisation and globalization, Traditional potters of Tamilnadu*, pp. 37-48
4. www.muguthese.com
5. Sreerangi *Economics of Labour in the Traditional Handicrafts Industries of Kerala*, p. 7.
6. Carla M. Sinopoli (1996), Ceramic Use and Ritual Practices in Hindu India
7. The Kumbaran of India, *International Journal of Frontier Missions,* vol. 14:3
8. *Hari D Goyal (2000), Impact Assessment Study* of Socio-*Economic Development Programmes – A case Study of Himachal Pradesh*
9. Radhika Vaidyanathan (2001), The Velar Makers of Ritual Terracotta, *Indian Folklife*, vol. 1, pp. 10-12 .
10. Srijan se Shakti (2001) Chinhat Pottery, Lucknow.
11. Lalitha Bomba (2002), *Techno-economic Survey of the Traditional Potter.*
12. Vasanth Shinde (2002) "Ethno-Arhalogical study of Pottery Manufacture", p. 10.
13. Archana Chok, *Pottery Manufacture in Kutch.*

14. Shailesh Kumar Singh (2005) "Living on the Edge - An Appraisal of Livelihoods in Rural Jharkhand", pp. 47-49.

15. Naresh Bhatnagar Chayaraj Meena and Suresh Babu (2005), "Potters Wheel Developmet—A Necessity for rural growth", *Journal of Rural Technology*, vol. 2, p. 46.

16. Nabakumar Duary (2007), "Traditional Hina Potters of Lower Assam", *Indian Journal of Traditional Knowledge*, vol 7(1), p. 98-102.

17. Suresh (2007), *Mitigating Health Risks in the Pottery Sector : Case Study in Kumbharwada,* Mumbai (India).

18. Daniel Paut (2007), *Evaluation Study of Rural Tourism Scheme.*

19. Bala Sirika (2008), *Socio-economic Status of Handicrafts Women.*

20. Charu Smith Guptha, "Clay-traditional material for making Handicrafts", *Indian journal of traditional knowledge*, vol 7(1), p. 116-124.

21. Pyare Lal (2009), Status of Youth Artisan in Bihar: Assessment of Potential of Artisans Sector for Generating Large Scale Self Employment in BIHAR, Bihar Institute of Economic Studies, p. 3.1 -6.1.

22. Parthasarathy, *The Pattern of Production and Market for Artisan Goods.*

23. I. Satya Sundaram, *Rural Development*, Himalaya Publishing House.

24. P S Sreenivas Naidu, "Socio-economic Condition of Artisan in Kurnool District".

25. Stephanson "Economics of Labour in the Traditional Handicrafts Industries of Kerala", p. 7.

CHAPTER

Rural Artisans : An Overview

Historical Perspective

An artisan constitutes an important segment of the rural economy, which provides livelihood opportunities to a majority of rural poor community. Artisans of India comprise of highly skilled traditional workforce, attached to varied operation in carpentry, blacksmith, goldsmith, stonesmith, copper/bronzesmith, masonry, pottery and cobbler.

Rural artisans used to assume a separate entity in the village life and used to provide effective support and servicing facilities for the economic activities like household tools and farm equipment and maintenance of the equipment in the village. In return they used to get a fixed share of the peasant's produce and raw material for producing the equipment and house hold things. At many places the village artisans were mainly *balutedars* and received rent-free land in return for the services they rendered. *Baluta* system, though fast disappearing, still remains in some of the villages of the district.

The rural artisan is a skilled worker in a traditional village craft who works on his own account. In most instances, the artisanship is primarily based on the existing resources of that particular area e.g. wood, leaves, minor forest produce, clay, stones etc. Most villages have an artisan population that creates different objects for functional purposes. From several studies done on the system of artisans industry in Pre-British period it appears that rural artisan also provided employment to landless laboures in their workshops and followed an ensured system of income distribution in the village society in its own old fashion way.[1]

Rural Cottage Industries and Artisan Products

Cottage industry is a specialized form of small scale industry where the production of the commodity takes place in the homes and the labor is supplied by the family members only. The machineries or means utilized for the production of the commodities generally are the common ones used at homes. The basic characteristic feature of cottage industry is that it is unorganized in nature and comes under the group of small scale industry type.

The commodities that are being produced by these industries are basically consumable ones and are produced through the utilization of the traditional techniques.

The cottage industries were both urban and rural in character. The urban handicrafts included quality textiles and other luxury goods for the aristocracy and the rural counterpart mainly consisted of black smithy, carpentry, pottery and weaving.

The rural/cottage industries are classified as:

- Pottery and ceramics
- Wood related — Match industry, carpentry, bamboo and canework and hand-made paper.
- Metalwares — Aluminum vessels, brassware, blacksmithy and agricultural tools.
- Leather — Leather processing.

- Chemicals — inks and dyes.
- Textiles — Handlooms, *polyvastra* and *khadi*.

Khadi and Village Industries Commission (KVIC)

The first and foremost industry that provides support to the rural artisans is the Khadi and Village Industries Commission of the Central Government, and Khadi and Village Industries Board of different State Governments.[2]

Khadi and Village Industries Commission is a statutory body established by an act of Parliament in April 1957 for the development of Khadi and Village Industries in India. Broad objectives for its establishment are social objective of providing employment, economic objective of producing saleable articles and the wider objective of creating self-reliance amongst the poor and building up of a strong rural community spirit. Wide range of activities including technical and financial support to the rural artisans generates employment to the unemployed youths presently.

KVIC provides assistance to khadi and village industries which are characterised by low capital intensity and ideally suited to manufacturing utility goods by using locally available resources. There are about 26 specified Village Industries such as village pottery, carpentry, blacksmithy, house hold aluminum utensils.

KVIC undertakes activities like skill improvement, transfer of technology, research and development and marketing in the process of generating employment/self-employment opportunities in rural areas.

Group Insurance Scheme for Khadi Artisans

Group Insurance Scheme for Khadi Artisans has been introduced with a view to provide safe and secure life to Khadi Artisan. The scheme covers all the spinners, weavers, pre-spinning artisans and post-weaving artisans engaged in khadi activity, associated with Khadi Institutions (NGOs) throughout the Country.

Contribution

Under the scheme, a yearly contribution of Rs. 200 is made per artisan out of which Rs. 25 is paid by the Artisan and rest is borne by Khadi Institution (NGO), CKVI and Social Security Fund of Government of India.

Financial Assistance

Table 2.1 shows the financial assistance available under the scheme.

Table 2.1. Financial Assistance for Insurance Scheme

Natural death	Rs 20,000
Death due to accidents	Rs 50,000
Permanent total disability (loss of two eyes / two limbs due to accident).	Rs 50,000
Permanent total disability (loss of one eye / one limb due to accident).	Rs 25,000
Educational Expenses in the form of scholarship upto two children from class 9th to 12th Std.	Rs 1,200 per annum

Sources: Khadi Village and Industries Commission, 2008-2009.

Awards for Khadi and Village Industries Artisans

Since Independence various steps have been taken for artisans' development. In 1963, the annual National Awards for Excellence in crafts was instituted. Outstanding craftsmen and weavers are conferred recognition through National Awards (every year) given away by the President of India. After setting up the scheme in 1965, 667 craftpersons/weavers have received National Awards.

The Khadi and Village Industries Commission has been working for the past 53 years. But, there is no such type of scheme to provide the State and National Award to the Gramodyog Shilpi/skill artisans, etc. who are excellent in development of process, design etc. and engaged in manufacturing of V.I. Products as these artisans' skill needs to be appreciated in KVI Sector. Award is to encourage the Gramodyog Shilpi/skill artisans for their good work in their respective areas for evolving good process in the rural Industrialization. Further ,this will set an example to other artisans who will improve their skillfullness to get such type of awards.

The financial implications under the Award Scheme have been worked out as under:

(A) Award Pattern (For Khadi & VI)

National level	:	Winner	—	Rs. 0.50 Lakhs
		Runner up	—	Rs. 0.25 Lakhs
State level	:	Winner	—	Rs. 0.10 Lakhs
		Runner up	—	Rs. 0.05 Lakhs

(B) Number of persons to be awarded

I. At National level: 10 in V.I. & 4 in Khadi = 14

II. At State level :

Under VI

Winners 5 Categories in 27 States	=	135
Runner up 5 Categories in 27 States	=	135
Total		270

Under Khadi

Winners 2 Categories in 27 States	=	54
up 2 Categories in 27 States	=	54
Total		108

(At State level 378 persons are to be awarded under Khadi & VI)

Workshed Scheme for Khadi Artisans

In order to facilitate and empower *khadi* spinners and weavers to chart out a sustainable path for growth, income generation and better work environment and to enable them to carry out their spinning and weaving work effectively 'Workshed Scheme for Khadi Artisans' was introduced in May 2008. Under this Scheme, financial assistance for construction of worksheds is provided to *khadi* artisans belonging to BPL category through the *khadi* institutions which the *khadi* artisans are associated with. Table 2.2 reveals the quantum of assistance for workshed

Table 2.2. Quantum of Assistance for Workshed

Component	Area per unit	Amount of Assistance
Individual Workshed	20 Square meters (approximately)	Rs. 25,000 or 75% of the cost of the workshed, whichever is less.
Group Worksheds (for a group of minimum 5 and maximum 15 khadi artisans)	15 Square meters perbeneficiary (approximately)	Rs. 15,000 per beneficiary of the group or 75% of the total cost of the project, whichever is less.

Source: Micro, Small and Medium Enterprises, Annual report 2008-09.

Besides promoting sale of *khadi* and village industries' products through its network of Khadi Gramodyog Bhavans (KGB) and Retail Sales Outlets, efforts are made to organise a number of exhibitions, in different parts of the country, as a cost effective publicity and market promotion instrument. During 2008-09, special efforts were made in this regard and a total of 144 exhibitions/events were organised in various parts of the country.

Khadi Artisans Welfare Trust Fund (KAWTF)

KAWTF is conceptually meant to be run on the lines of a Provident Fund. The Membership of KAWTF is mandatory for all khadi and polyvastra producing institutions affiliated to KVIC and State KVIBs. All the Institutions categorized as A+, A, B and C are eligible to join the Trust Fund. This Trust Fund has been functioning in 20 States and the State Government concerned manages this Trust Fund.

Khadi and Village Industries provide various facilities to the artisans/entrepreneurs for the development and promotion of village industries and to bring qualitative improvement in the traditional crafts.

Khadi and Village Industries Board (KVIB)

Khadi and Village Industries Board is a statutory body constituted by the Act IX of 1957 of Legislative Assembly. The Board is vested with the responsibility of organising, promoting and developing Khadi and Village Industries in the State.

Khadi and Village Industries Board was constituted in the year 1959 for encouraging and promoting Khadi and Village Industries thereby for providing employment in rural areas.

The object of the Board is to provide employment to the rural artisans/entrepreneurs, at their home thereby arresting the migration of rural population to urban areas and to develop the Khadi and Village Industries in rural areas in collaboration with like-minded agencies engaged in rural development work.

The Board has been doing its service for the development of Khadi and Village Industries in this State particularly in rural areas for the past five decades. The Board is the authority to register Co-operative Societies formed by like minded people under the Co-operative Societies Act to develop Khadi and Village Industries. Through these Co-operative Societies the board also promotes Khadi and Village Industries and thereby provides maximum possible level of employment opportunities to the rural artisans.

The State and Central Governments provide financial support in the form of grants to the Board for supply of beehives to the Rural folks and Tribals in hill areas, for modernization of looms to weavers and other equipments, to village artisans.

The various schemes implemented by the Board through the financial assistance of the State and Central Governments are given in Table 2.3

Table 2.3. Financial Assistance of the State and Central Governments

Name of the Scheme	Amount assisted (Rs. in lakhs)	No. of beneficiaries
Integrated Tribal Development Programme	562.14	8,397
Western Ghats Development Programme for the welfare of artisans	121.36	5,884
Hill Area Development Programme exclusively for the development of the artisans in and around the Nilgris district	213.36	6,107
Special Central Assistance for Scheduled Castes	2707.00	37,317

Source: Khadi Village Industries Board 2008-09.

In order to perform the above duties, the Board receives funds from the State Government as grant under plan and from the KVIC as loan and grant. Financial assistance is also being recommended through other financial institutions. The schemes of the Board were implemented through Co-operative Societies, registered institutions, individuals and departmental units of the Board. These units were started with a view to provide regular employment to rural artisans within their local premises.

Council for Advancement of People's Action and Rural Technology (CAPART)

Council for Advancement of People's Action and Rural Technology (CAPART) is an autonomous body registered under the Societies Registration Act, 1860 and is functioning under the aegis of the Ministry of Rural Development. CAPART is involved in catalysing and co-coordinating the emerging partnership between Voluntary Organisations and the Government of India for sustainable development of Rural Areas.

The aim of the CAPART is to provide training to the rural poor artisans to raise their skills, productivity and income. So far 104 projects have been implemented benefiting about 4221 rural poor artisans for which Rs.1.78 crore has been extended as assistance to the implementing Voluntary Organisations and Provides marketing support to the rural artisans and promotes their goods as exhibition-cum-sales fair under the brand name of SARAS will display a wide range of products manufactured by the rural artisans, craftsmen and beneficiaries of Self-help Groups from all over the country. It creates a unique platform for developing linkages with the buyers and customers and also provides opportunity to deal directly with the buyers avoiding the middle men.[3]

District Industries Centres (DICS)

Governments - both Central and State, have in the past taken a number of measures for the development of small and village industries, but the actual achievements have been far below the expectations. Also the focus of attention for industrial development was mainly on large cities and State capitals to the neglect of district areas. In addition, multiplicity of institutions involved in small industries development and complicated systems and procedures made the job of promoting the industrial units an uphill task for small entrepreneurs. Hence, it was felt necessary to establish a development agency which could provide all services and facilities to village and small industries under one roof. Accordingly, the DICs were established in May 1978 in order to cater to the needs of small units.

Each district has a DIC at its headquarters. The main responsibility of DIC is to act as the chief coordinator or multifunctional agency in respect of various government departments and other agencies. The prospective small entrepreneurs would get all assistance from DIC for setting up and running an industry in rural areas.

The District Industries Centre is functioning mainly with the aim of promoting, facilitating and developing industrial growth in the territory and to develop the skill in order to create better employment opportunities and to boost the livelihood of rural people who have contributed a significant share to the exports. Some of the main activities of DIC in handicraft sector are to provide loan for handicrafts artisans and to assist the artisans for marketing their products.

Small Industries Products Promotion Organisation (SIPPO)

Small Industries Products Promotion Organisation has been promoted as a vehicle that will reach such government programmes to rural entrepreneurs. It has been launched with an objective to promote Small Scale, Village and Rural Industries through capacity building.

SIPPO has promoted many Entrepreneurs in various fields like Handicrafts, Floriculture, Essential Oils, Cosmetic Industries, Granite Industry, Pharmaceuticals, Medicinal Plants and aromatic plants cultivation and distillations food processing industries, eco-friendly industries through various training programs, seminars, workshops and exhibitions organized in various Districts of Tamil Nadu and other States.

SIPPO is a Nodal Agency and its services has been utilized by different Ministries like Ministry of Food Processing, Ministry of Textiles, Ministry of MSME, KVIC, District Industries Centre, and National Centre for Jute Diversification, DRDA, Gulf of Mannar Bio Sphere Reserve Trust, Ministry of Agriculture, Ministry of Science and Technology, Ministry of Commerce, and Ministry of Agro and Rural Industries.

SIPPO provides backward linkages in design enhancement, product diversification, and financial institutional linkage for accessing credits and better quality and standardization practices that are best suited for the changing market needs to artisan's communities.

It trains the entrepreneurs through skill upgradation training programmes and conducts seminars, workshops and conferences on specific sectors in the different parts of the country. Offers craft-oriented certificate courses through its Academy.

Facilitates the supply of machineries, equipment and other accessories to entrepreneurs. Facilitates supply of raw material to Small Scale, Agro, Rural and Village Industrial units in SIPPO clusters. Also offers marketing guidance to these units. Conducts product promotion exhibitions and buyer-seller meets at different locations.

National Bank for Agricultural and Rural Development (Nabard)

The NABARD is an apex institution, accredited with all matters concerning policy, Planning and operation in the field of credit for agriculture and other economic activities in rural areas in India.

NABARD is established as a development Bank, in terms of the Preamble of the NABARD Act, "of providing and regulating Credit and other facilities for the promotion and development of agricultural, small scale industries, cottage and village industries, handicrafts and other rural crafts and other allied economic activities in rural areas with a view to promoting integrated rural development and securing prosperity of rural areas and for matters connected therewith or incidental thereto."

NABARD was set up with a mission to promote sustainable and equitable agriculture and rural development through effective credit support, related services, institution building and other innovative initiatives. Primarily its objectives are to:

(*i*) serve as an apex financing agency;

(*ii*) take measures towards institution building for improving absorptive capacity of the credit delivery system, including monitoring, formulation of rehabilitation schemes, restructuring of credit institutions, training of personnel, etc.,

(*iii*) co-ordinate the rural financing activities of all institutions engaged in developmental work at the field level and liaise with Government of India, state governments, Reserve Bank of India (RBI) and other national level institutions concerned with policy formulation; and

(*iv*) undertake monitoring and evaluation of projects refinanced by it.

The NABARD being an Apex Development Bank promotes agriculture and rural development through refinance support to all banks for investment credit and to Co-operatives and RRBs for production credit. The objective of providing refinance to eligible institutions is to supplement their resources for delivering credit for agriculture,cottage & village industries, SSIs , rural artisans, etc., thus influencing the quantum of lending in consonance with the policy of Government of India.

The NABARD's refinance is available to State Co-operative Agriculture and Rural Development Banks (SCARDBs), State Co-operative Banks (SCBs), Regional Rural Banks (RRBs), Commercial Banks (CBs) and other financial institution approved by RBI. While the ultimate beneficiaries of investment credit can be individuals, partnership concerns, companies, State-owned corporations or co-operative societies, production credit is generally given to individuals.

These organisations help the rural folk in

- Technology upgradation
- Organisation for the artisans

- Getting credit from institutions
- Procurement and Supply of the materials
- Establishment of worksheds, where the artisans can work and use upgraded technology and equipment
- Domestic marketing through retails outlets, and
- Export marketing wherever possible.

These incentives have helped the artisans to stay in their profession and also profitably practice the trade known to them for ages without migrating to the urban areas.

Rural Artisans

Artisans have a vital role to play in the economic development of the country. The artisans formed the base of industrial activity in India during the pre-Colonial and the early Colonial periods. They seemed to enjoy a reasonably good social status in society in ancient period.

Artisans traditionally belonged to professions of blacksmith, goldsmith, stone carvers, carpenters, weavers, basket making, leather workers, metal workers, potters.

The artisans have been significant actor or pillar of the rural society. Artisans mostly utilise locally available resources for manufacturing process, servicing of a product or an activity and they are engaged in procuring, a wide variety of the products like carpets, brassware, earthenware, textile and artistic pieces for the local people. Most villages have an artisan population that creates different objects for functional purposes. The growth and promotion of these artisan units greatly depends upon fulfilment of their needs and requirements.

Blacksmith

Every village has its blacksmith who produces and repairs agricultural implements and domestic articles. It was the hereditary occupation of the lohars. In rural areas the occupation is still with the hereditary artisans. In urban areas, however, it is open to any one trained in the art of blacksmiths.

Blacksmith make various agricultural implements like spades, axes, furrows, sickles, field tools etc., and domestic articles like flat pans and frying pans. The impact of industrial change has not affected its technique of production. Even today they continue to produce the same articles as were produced in the past. Tools required are anvil, hammer, pincers, bellows, chisel, cutters and nails. Each Blacksmith usually possesses a set of such tools.

The iron sheets from which these articles are made are brought from outside. Middlemen often supply the artisan with capital necessary for buying iron sheets and other accessories and purchase their products in lieu of repayment. This sometimes reduces the artisans to the status of ordinary wage earners carrying on repair work and production work on piece rate basis as per the orders received through their financiers

Investment amount is usually borrowed by the artisans at high rate of interest from local money-lenders. These artisans are illiterate and do not favour any improvement in the technique of production. And even if they desire they do not possess the necessary financial ability to introduce the changes required in the technique.

Goldsmith

A goldsmith is generally a pious person, doing his artistic work with gold as a cottage industry, making gold and silver ornaments with hand at the sit-out of his house or in a tiny shop. The ornaments which are popular in Tamil Nadu are *mangal sutra*, (*thali* chain), *oddiyaanam* (gold waist belt), *jimikki* (eardrop), and *mookuthi* (nose-petal) and gold bangles etc. They were traditionally crafted and finished with great dexterity. Ornaments worth several thousand rupees are handed over to goldsmith just out of trust for making, with no acknowledgement for the transaction taking place. It is based on mutual trust and long-standing relationship. Their skill can be recognized from the jewels adorning the statues of various gods in Hindu temples. Goldsmiths are generally located in a row of tiny shops one after another in specific streets – whether they are in towns or cities.

The goldsmith normally takes one-week to ten days time to deliver for an order. There used to be a small jewellery shop by the side of the goldsmiths, which later became goldsmiths sitting by the side of small jewellery shops. In either way, the goldsmith had a place. In the former case goldsmiths assumed significance and in the latter case it is the jewellery shop that assumed significance.. After liberalization where jewellery showrooms have assumed the prime-place, the traditional goldsmiths go there seeking employment

Stone Carvers

Stone carving is one traditional skill handed down from generation to generation. They learn by drawing and making a variety of carving works in stone. In the opinion of the sculptors, being and practicing as a sculptor requires concentration, patience, dedication, and more significantly a spiritualistic approach, as mostly these deal with sculpting figures of deities.

The quality of the material is one extremely important part of the sculptural process. The quality of stone, its maturity, texture and colour are important for stone carvers

Some of the stone carvers own small worksheds where they make sculptures. Some of the stone carvers own big workshed (master stone carvers) where stone carvers are employed for a wage. Stone carvers work on a soft stone for carving deities while a hard stone is suitable for making temple top, pillars, roof, *mandapam* (hall) etc.

Nowadays, machines have been introduced for cutting stone and polishing. Use of machine for cutting is considered reducing the drudgery. Although use of polishing machine saves on the time one has to spend in manual polishing, it generates a lot of dust which is hazardous to the lungs. One can understand the volume of work being handled by stone carvers by looking up the frequency of procuring raw stones, and the frequency of sending across a truckload of finished products.

Availing bank loan is a long-drawn process and so, sculptors avoid seeking financial assistance from the local banks. They pledge jewels and borrow from informal money lenders to make investments on stones and to pay truck fare.

Carpenters

Every large village has one or two families of carpenters known as sutars. Formerly these artisans worked on *baluta* system, and a share in the agricultural produce was given to them for their services. The *baluta* system has now almost disappeared and the artisans are paid in cash. In rural area number of carpenters make and repair agricultural implements and bullock-carts. In urban area they are engaged in furniture-making and construction of houses.

Carpenters make and repair furniture of daily use, viz., chairs, cupboards, benches, cradles and agricultural tools, handlooms and warping frames required for the looms. A carpenter's tools are saw, plaining machine, foot rule, hammer, nails, screws, chisel etc.

Lack of capital for the purchase of wood and adequate training facilities are the main difficulties experienced by the cottage workers. Middlemen or moneylenders often advance capital. Some of the artisans are engaged by building contractors and *karkhandars* on wage basis. The wage depends upon their skill and the type of the work involved. But with the expansion of the tyre borne traffic the bullock-cart has lost its importance as a means of travel and this has indirectly affected the carpentry industry. In spite of this situation employment in the industry has remained more or less constant with the increasing tempo of the building activity and there has been an increase in the demand for the services of this class of artisans along with that of blacksmiths and bricklayers.

Weavers

Handloom-weaving is another premier cottage industry. The artistic skills of the traditional handloom weaver are caste based and tradition-oriented. Hand-weaving was done in cotton, silk and wool and in a combined thread of cotton and silk. Handloom-weaving was mainly confined to hereditary weaving communities like *salis* and *koshtis* and wool and cotton fabrics were produced

Raw materials such as cotton yarn of different counts and dyeing materials are imported from Mumbai. Cotton yarn is supplied by co-operative societies to those who are their members. Others obtain it from local market. The market for the product is generally local. The poverty of these artisans often forces them to sell their products at the prices which are sometimes below the cost of production.

Gradually with the establishment of cotton textile, handloom weaving suffered considerably. Weavers do not have adequate capital resources for investment in the business. Most of them, therefore, resort to borrowing and sell their goods on retail or on wholesale basis on their own account immediately when the production is over. Handloom artisans weave the cloth and members of their family help them in preliminary operations. The working hours in the industry are from morning till evening and holiday is observed on the *amavasya,* the last day of the dark half. A weaver produces about 20 such *saris* in a month.

Basket Making

Basket making is a hereditary occupation of the burud community. People from Burud caste has traditional occupation of preparing articles from bamboo. Burud is name specific to particular States like Maharashtra. Burud is derived from a Sanskrit word *Buruda* which means a basket-maker, mat-maker.

In Karnataka people with similar occupation are called *Medar,* while in Madhaya Pradesh they are called as *Basor.* Similarly they are spread in different parts of India. Their social status varies from State to State.

In a day two adult members of a family make five or six winnowing fans from one bamboo or a kanagi from two bamboos. Men usually take out bamboo strips and the womenfolk make these articles. The cost of producing six winnowing fans is about Rs. 1.87 including cost of raw materials and wages of labour.

Bamboo-strips are taken out with a sickle and wetted. Moistening the strip makes the weaving of the baskets easy. The products are mostly sold locally. There are no co-operative societies for these artisans.

A few artisans who follow the occupation as a permanent one stock the bamboo in advance for the rainy season. The business is dull during the rainy season. Bamboos which grow in abundance in the forests of the district are mainly used for making these articles. The tools required are knife and cutter, which the artisans purchase without any difficulty.

An artisan who invests Rs. 200 in the industry can keep a stock of bamboos for future use and it does not require much investment. But the amount so invested is usually borrowed from merchant financiers at a considerably higher rate of interest which he cannot afford.

There has not been any change in the technique of their production during the last fifty years. They use the same tools they used 57 years ago. They are also backward and comparatively illiterate. They live in the same huts as they were living before. Nor do they possess any landed property. If an artisan intends to expand his occupation he has to resort to the money-lender who grants him necessary capital at exorbitant rate of interest. The industry does not yield him income sufficient to make his both ends meet.

Leather Working

Leather-working is one of the old cottage industries. A few shoemakers are found in every village. Shoemaking is a hereditary occupation of the Chambhars who make shoes, sandals and chappals of various designs. Nowadays persons other than Chambhars are also found to be taking to this industry. It produces the footwear in common use like chappals, shoes, etc., buckets for drawing water from wells, leather straps and belts and other goods required by the agriculturist or the artisan. In towns the leather workers also prepare leather bags, purses, etc. They make and sell a variety of leather articles.

The tools commonly used for leather-working are the sewing machine, rapiers, leather cutters, hammer, wooden block, nails etc. Hence, the tools used and the process followed are age-old and the hereditary training still predominates. The raw materials chiefly consist of tanned and dyed leather, rubber soles, polish etc. Tanned leather is procured from the district and is supplied by the local tanning industry. The artisans face severe competition from the footwear companies whose products are of a superior design and finish. In rural areas, artisans work as a family unit. In urban areas they are in the employment of big establishments. Some of them combine tanning with leather working.

A good artisan with the help of an assistant makes a pair of shoes in a day. The cost of producing a pair of shoes is Rs. 14 including wages and cost of raw materials. Most of the products are sold locally. In urban areas there are establishments which employ two or three artisans. In rural areas artisans do not possess separate establishments nor do they employ outside labour. They work in their own houses and produce leather articles which are required locally.

An ordinary artisan requires. Rs. 100 as an investment in the industry. Further expansion of the establishment depends upon the capital available. In urban areas sometimes more than Rs. 5,000 is invested in an establishment producing leather goods. In urban areas many artisans are employed on piece wages.

Potters

Pottery

Pottery is a hereditary industry of *kumbhar* who produce earthen wares and toys during festival days. Nowadays earthen wares and toys are not much used by the people as they were used before the introduction of copper and brass wares. They are mostly used by poor people who cannot afford to have brass and copper utensils.

The potter's equipment mainly consists of the traditional potter's wheel, moulds, pickaxes, ghamelas, and kiln to bake the pots. Horse dung, clay and coal ash are the raw materials required. Fallen dry leaves of banyan and *pimpal* trees are used for baking. The village potter makes the traditional village pottery like *gadgis, madakis, ranjan* (round earthen pots) and *thalis* (dishes). The making of these articles involves a curious process. There is the potter's wheel which rotates to give the proper shape for these articles with the helping hand of the potter synchronising with the movements of the wheel. The pots are dried in the sun and then baked in the kiln to make them perfect. They are then glazed and polished. At some places the potters make idols of Goddess Gauri and God Ganesh during Ganapati festival and *sugadi* (small round clay pots) during *Makarsankrant*. Some of them also make earthen toys.

Potters Community

In India, potters usually live in settlements in interior villages. These potters settlements belong to various communities and are known by different caste names in different places such as *Kumbaran, Kusavan, Adi Andhra,* Tamil cultured *Kumbaran, Mannudayan, Kulala, Andhur Nair, Andhra Nair, Velan, Pandy Velan, Odan* and *Urali Kurumban*. They are communities engaged in pottery occupation. Most of these potter settlements are located in river basins or near to paddy fields. This is obviously related to raw material availability. In each settlement there will be a few kilns, which are used by all of them irrespective of their ownership. The work area is mostly located adjacent to the homes. In several places the interior of the houses are also used to keep the pots either baked or raw (for drying). In certain places, a few potters are found living in their kiln shed itself.

Potters complain that the revenue authorities do not issue caste certificate as *Kumbaran*. Instead, the authorities issue caste certificate as *Kusava*. So they have accepted *'Kusava'* as their caste name. They still believe that there is no caste called *Kusava*.

Livelihood Pattern of Potters

Pottery was a family occupation and it still remains so. However, a snap shot view of outsiders to potters residential area makes one think of women involved more in making the pottery articles. The role of men seems to be at the beginning by making arrangements for procuring the right kind of clay, and at the end arranging the made-pottery articles in the kiln for baking. Preparing the clay and giving shape to it seems to be with women, off and on joined by men.

These days, due to the improved awareness level on the importance of education, children from potters' families are also sent to school. But, many boys and girls, before and after school-hours try their hands in making pottery articles and help their parents increase the quantity produced. That which these children start as a fun, dirtying their hands with wet-mud eventually results in picking up a livelihood skill. Similarly, even the elderly women in the house engage themselves during seasonal requirements such as making karthic lamps. There is an admirable family dynamics that operates in potters' families in the process of carrying out their work for earning a living. Potters usually locate themselves in a place that is away from the main village considering factors such as availability of water and spacious place to sun dry their articles. It is also in a way keeping the main community away from the kiln smoke, which otherwise is a usual complaint of the mainstream community about the potters that the potters pollute the environment with kiln-smoke.

As far as sale of pottery articles is concerned, taking pottery articles to long distance for sales seems to be with the men, whereas taking articles to weekly shandy at the villages in the neighbourhood seems to be with the women. Where potters work on a cooperative basis, the cooperative society makes arrangement for sale of pottery articles, including the transport to the marketplace. In the recent years, there are also business persons who buy pottery articles from potters and send lorry loads to places such as Kerala. They also offer money in advance to help the production take place.

Welfare of Potters

The Government is providing various welfare benefits to potters by forming a welfare board for them. With a view to helping them, 500 electrically operated potter's wheels were be provided free of cost.

In the thousands of years pottery has been practiced, one of the farthest reaching innovations was the introduction of electric-powered potter's wheels (pottery wheels). Electric potter's wheels allow potters to produce volumes of work faster than before. Electric wheels are also lighter and much more easily moved than wheels.

The electric wheel, replacing the manually operated and labour intensive wheel, nearly looks like a small grinder in shape with a rotating wooden plank attached to its middle. The electrical wheel facilitates potters to concentrate more on their work, as they can now use both the hands for moulding the piece without any extra care for manual rotation of the wheel.

Toolkits

Once the clay has been roughly moulded by hand or on a wheel, it has to be refined and decorated. Then only pottery tools come into the picture. They are meant for various purposes, and may be made of a variety of materials.

The tools used in pottery are

- Shaping tools,
- Throwing tools,
- Trimming tools and
- Texturing tools.

These pottery decorating tools are often available in sets. These collections of tools for pottery vary in price depending upon quality and the numbers of tools. Pottery tool sets are available for both beginners and professionals. While some of the tools are used as aids in the moulding of the clay, others are used once the clay has partially hardened. At this stage, it is possible to carve and burnish the pottery. Tools are also used once the pottery has been hardened.[4]

The total number of rural artisans and potters in Madurai Revenue Division are given in Table 2.4

Table 2.4. Rural Artisans and Potters in Madurai Revenue Division

Rural artisans	Potters
6194	925

Source: District Industries Center, Madurai 2008-2009.

Special Schemes For Rural Artisans

Artisan Credit Card (ACC) Scheme

The objective of the ACC Scheme is to provide adequate and timely assistance from the banking institution to the artisans to meet their credit requirement of both investment need as well as working capital, in a flexible and cost effective manner. All artisans involved in production/manufacturing process are eligible. No collateral security is required for availing credit card. Beneficiaries will be issued with a photo card indicating sanctioned limit and validity period of credit facility. Credit limit would be fixed based on assessment of working capital requirements. A maximum credit limit of Rs. 2 lakh shall be provided. The limit could normally be valid for a period of three years subject to annual review by the bank.

Life Insurance Scheme for Artisans

The scheme will be taken up through LIC. The corporation shares premium for such schemes meant for the bottom strata of the population, which includes artisans as well. The annual premium of Rs. 200 will be equally shared by the LIC and the Directorate of Industries contributing Rs. 100 each. The artisans do not have to pay anything for getting this insurance coverage which have following benefits. Table 2.5 exhibits the insurance coverage available for the artisans.

Table 2.5. Life Insurance Scheme for Artisans

Benefits to life insured	Condition precedent
Rs. 30,000.00	On normal death
Rs. 75,000.00	On accidental death/permanent disability
Rs. 37,500.00	On Partial disability

Source: Handicrafts annual report 2008-2009.

In addition to the above benefits, a monthly stipend of Rs. 100 each is also provided to two students in the family of the insured artisans. The proposed scheme will cover artisans between the age group of 35 to 60 years. It is estimated that around 8.00 lacs artisans are under this age bracket, who need to be covered. The other eligibility criteria will be Artisans Identity Card being issued by the Development Commissioner (Handicrafts), Ministry of Textiles, GOI/the State Government.

Pension Scheme for Distinguished Artisans

The scheme will be operated in the entire State. Under the scheme a monthly pension of Rs. 1,000 is envisaged to each artisan honoured with Shilp Guru citation of the GOI/ National Handicrafts Award/State Merit Award and who also have attained a minimum age of 60 years. In first year of the 11th Five-year Plan 100 such artisans are expected to be alive and eligible. Mastercraft persons unable to work due to old age and infirmity are eligible for pension. Various craftpersons are receiving pension at present.

Social Security Schemes

Social security and welfare of artisans is another area which is being given special attention. As a welfare measure for artisans, various schemes like providing assistance for construction of Worksheds, Workshed-cum-Housing, and Group Insurance Scheme have been introduced since 1994-95. However, based on the recommendations of the Sub Group for Ninth Plan, these schemes have been further modified to suit the requirement of the artisans. These schemes have become very popular measures for providing security net to craftsmen. In the coming years, all the state handicrafts corporation and leading NGOs will be encouraged to avail the financial assistance from the Government and bring more and more craftspersons under this security net.

Training and Assistance—Rural Artisans

Training for Handicraft Artisans

Training is given for upgradation of skills of the existing craftpersons as well as to unskilled ones with a view to expanding production base and for crafts having high potential for economic growth and for revival of languishing crafts.

Being rich in a number of handicrafts, the state has great scope to attract new entrepreneurs for adopting handicrafts for self-employment. Training for skill development for the younger generation is proposed to be provided under the National and State Awardee Craftsmen/Shilp Guru and other renowned Craftsmen in case of non-availability of National/ State Awardees/Shilp Guru in a district. Such trainers will be known as Master Craftsmen. The training will be provided within the household of such Master Craftsmen under their strict and personal guidance to 10 persons in each centre under Guru-Shishya Parampara. In each year of the five-year plan 30 centres will be run for the duration of six months. A stipend of Rs. 500 per month will be paid to each trainee and Rs. 4000 per month as honorarium to the Master Craftsmen and Rs. 1000 per month as Raw material. Through these centers 300 persons will be benefited each year directly besides the 30 Master Craftsmen engaged as trainers. In the entire Five-year Plan period 1500 skilled artisans will enter into the field and create further employment opportunities to around 3000 persons, besides 150 Master Craftsmen.

Design Workshops for Export Market

Although handicraft export accounts for 60% of total exports from the State, this is almost limited to traditional designs which need a change to suit the requirements of fast changing market. In order to meet this challenge, design development workshops will be organized in main clusters of handicraft such as Moradabad, Varanasi, Lucknow, Agra, Firozabad etc. Designers of International repute will be invited through Export Promotion Council for Handicrafts, New Delhi and other sources for need-based workshops necessary to cover up the course content. Annually 14 workshops shall be organized covering 15-20 workers each, which will cost Rs. 21,00,000 each and Rs. 105,00,000 for the Five-year Plan.

Presently there is a shortage of skilled designers for export market; the exporters employ unskilled/semi-skilled persons who get trained while working in the establishment. Besides the proposed design workshops as above, additional workshops shall be arranged on demand from such exporters to create further job opportunities. It is expected that 200 workers for such sponsored workshops will be available in each year of the five year plan period which will require additional expenditure of Rs. 15 lacs annually to an aggregate of Rs. 75 lacs for the five year plan period.

It is expected that 15-20 crafts persons will be benefited in each workshop. On an average 250 craftsmen will be benefited each year through regular workshops and another 200 from sponsored workshops. These workshops will directly benefit 450 skilled designers.[5]

Problems of Rural Artisans

Accommodation

The artisans carry out their production activity at their houses. Most of the artisans, especially weavers and potters expressed that they are not having sufficient accommodation facility for their activities. Housing is a physical concept which determines the extent of civilization, sociological and economic advancement.

Lack of Improved Tools and Technology

Some artisans expressed "Tools and Technology" as their problem and more artisans have expressed that they are not having modern tools for their modern produce. Modern technology has enabled machines to imitate even the most intricate designs that were once the exclusive domain of the artisans, developed and perfected over centuries and passed down from generation to generation. Any form of innovation implies an element of risk and investment of capital. Given that most Indian artisans live on the margin of subsistence, they have virtually no reserves to invest in technological innovation (physical capital). The artisan's incredibly low income also helps to keep production costs low, and product prices competitive.

Lack of Financial Support

There is reluctance at the financial institutions at local branch level or procedural delay on account of lengthy paper work to provide financial assistance to the craft people. Artisans sometimes have to pay bribe even to get subsidies from the government.

Inadequate Infrastructure

A few artisans have expressed that there is lack of infrastructural facilities for their activities. The infrastructure with which rural artisans produce their handicraft is quite inadequate in comparison with what there should be in order to satisfy the consumer demand.

Lack of Working Capital and Easier Access to Credit

Lack of finance and cash flow is almost always the crux of craft people's problems. It is what restricts the economic development and the well being of artisans and their families. Inability to access government funds forces them to take loans from local middlemen and moneylenders at exorbitant rates of interest. The yoke of their debts to these middlemen and moneylender make many Indian crafts people into a form of bonded labour. As more than 90 per cent of rural artisan households are landless, they have minimal resources to mortgage or use as collateral for a loan. In such situations informal credit plays a critical role in the production and expansion of artisan's enterprise.

Lack of Access of Key Markets

The rural artisans belong to lowest rungs of the caste hierarchy knowing only how to create handicrafts as means of livelihood to support their families in the hard conditions in the backward regions of the country. But, they might not be good at skills to market them in the remunerative markets in bigger towns and cities.

Production Problems

Rural artisans lack guidance in product design and development based on the understanding of the demand of the market. Even when they know what has to be done, in most of the cases they do not have adequate means to do so.

Remedial Measures for Rural Artisans

Awareness Generation Camps

Awareness generation camps should be organised by various agencies associated with the rural development, particularly by the financial institutions. Institutions like National Bank for Agricultural and Rural Development (NABARD), District Cooperative Banks, District Industries Centres, Khadi and Village Industries Commission (KVIC), etc. could be approached for this purpose.

Training of Artisans

Arrangements should be made for providing trainings to the artisans through appropriate institutions. Training institutions should be involved in training the artisans with the main purpose of upgrading skills to enable them to handle jobs requiring better skills.

Financial Loans to the Artisans

A majority of artisans in this Cluster are tiny and marginal and needfinancial loans. But they are not able to avail themselves of different schemes of banks basically because of their inability to fulfill the conditions of the banks for granting loans. The banks and other financial institutions should modify their rules and regulations, including collateral requirements, so that small artisans of this area could also get the benefit of loan facilities.

Information Centre

Artisans are in need of setting-up of Information Centre to access information on marketing, technology-up gradation, and training institutions along with generating awareness about different schemes of Central and State governments for the benefits of rural people in general, and rural artisans in particular.[6]

Conclusions

Government should come forward to educate the artisans about attractive incentives and give wide publicity about developmental programmes of their activities.

REFERENCES

1. S.S.Sonanki and V.K.Gupta, *"Technological upgradation and the prospect of rural development"*, Deep and Deep Publications Pvt, Ltd., p. 204-213.
2. T P Gopal Swamy, "Rural Marketing Environment", Wheeler Publishing.
3. U C Mathu, *Rural Marketing Text and Cases,* Excel Publishing.

4. Dr. G. Palanidurai, *Decentralisation and globalization, Traditional potters of Tamil Nadu"*, p. 37-48.

5. Khadi Village Industries and Commission, *Annual Report 2008-2009.*

6. P Malaiyandi, "Development of rural artisans a case study", *Kurushetra*, Vol. XXXIII, No. 11, p. 18.

CHAPTER

Socio-Economic Conditions of Potters

Introduction

The socio-economic condition is the position occupied by the individual with reference to the prevailing average standards of the community. The societal position of an individual is judged by the indicators like education and involvement in leadership activities and the economic position of a person is assessed by the type of house, income and savings. The economic progress depends on the occupational status and the income derived from these sources.[1]

Pottery is one of the oldest technical trades in the history of human beings and nothing has changed in this trade, as far as the production technology is concerned. The socio-economic condition of the section of the society is very poor. Almost all of them are producing traditional earthenwares/ pots which have very low demand in the present society.

social status of potters is very low and the attitude of the mainstream society towards them is always negative. Potters maintain their own special type of social condition and are hesitant to mingle with the outer world. Potters are mainly depending on their traditional occupation for their income and it is observed that the potters are educationally and economically backward and remain away from the rest of society.[2]

In this chapter an attempt is made to analyse the:

- profile of the potters.
- earnings and expenditure.
- sources of savings.
- sources of borrowings.
- satisfaction level of potters.

Gender of the Potters

Gender is the socially constructed roles, behaviour activities and attributes that a particular society considers appropriate for men and women. Gender is a lens through which to examine roles and responsibilities of men and women and it helps in analysing the constraints faced by opportunities. Gender is a very important and useful dividing variable to classify the potters. To study the socio economic condition, the potters are classified on the basis of gender to know the extent of male-female participation. Table 3.1 and Fig. 3.1 show the gender wise classification of the potters.

Table 3.1. Gender-wise Classification

Gender	Number of potters	Percentage
Male	67	55.83
Female	53	44.17
Total	**120**	**100.00**

Source: Primary Data

From Table 3.1 it is inferred, that out of 120 selected potters male accounted for 58.83 per cent and remaining 44.17 per cent are female.

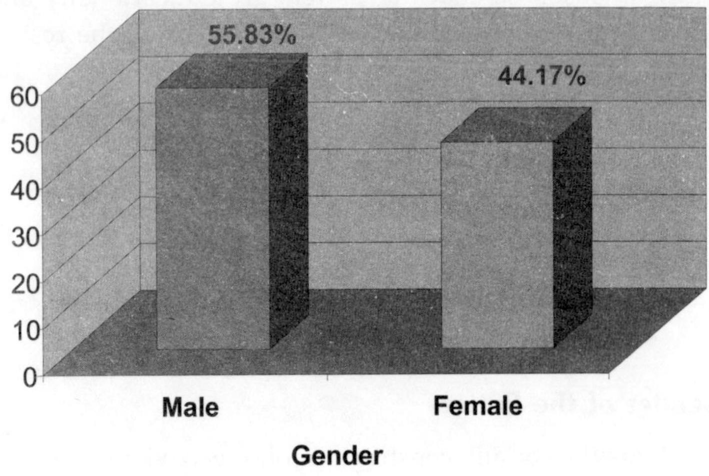

Fig. 3.1. Gender-wise Classification

Age of the Potters

Age factor which indicates a change in the nature of employment and also the need to find out the extent of the experiences and skills they have gained through pottery work.[3] Table 3.2 and Fig. 3.2 show the age-wise classification of the potters.

Table 3.2. Age-wise Classification

Age	Number of potters	Percentage
Less than 20 years	8	6.67
20-40 years	43	35.83
40-60 years	49	40.83
Above 60 years	20	16.67
Total	**120**	**100.00**

Sources: Primary Data

Table 3.2 and Fig. 3.2 depict that, out of 120 potters 40.83 percentage belong to the age group of 40-60years. In the age group of 20-40 years, there are forty three potters (35.83%). The other 20 (16.67%) falls under the age group of above 60 years. Only eight potters (6.67%) are below the age of twenty.

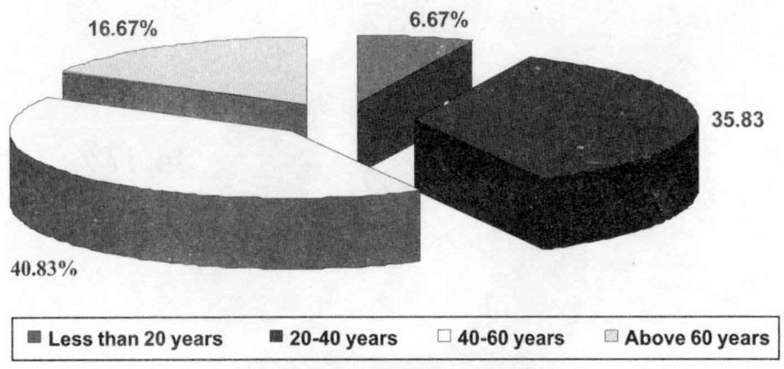

Fig. 3.2. Age-wise Classification

Educational Qualifications

Education plays a vital role in the development of any trade or occupation and also helps in the socio economic upliftment of the family. Table 3.3 and Fig. 3.2 show the educational status of the potters.

Table 3.3. Education- Wise Classification

Level of education	Number of potters	Percentage
No formal education	41	34.17
Primary education	56	46.67
High school	16	13.33
Higher secondary	7	5.83
Total	**120**	**100.00**

Sources: Primary Data

From Table 3.3 and Fig. 3.3 it is observed that majority of the potters (46.67%) have completed only primary education.

The percentage of the sample potters who have completed high school is 13.33 per cent and only seven (5.83%) of the total potters have finished their higher secondary education. It is significant to note that 34.17 per cent of the potters have no formal education.

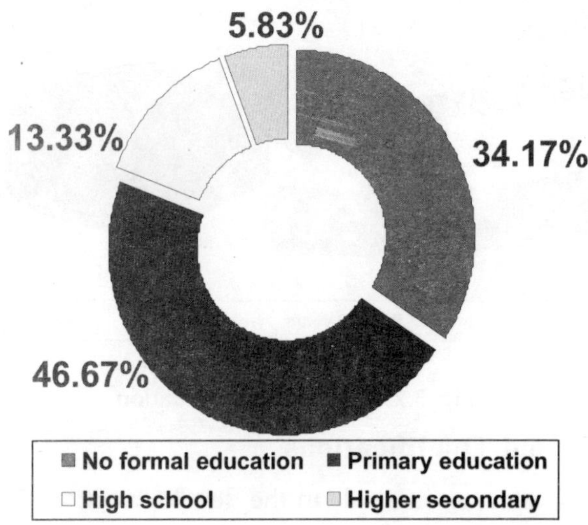

Fig. 3.3. Educational Status of the Potters

Marital Status of the Potters

Marital status of the potters mainly influence the expenditure pattern of the family. It is a significant factor which influences the satisfaction level of the pottery work. Table 3.4 and Fig. 3.4 enumerate the marital status of the potters.

Table 3.4. Marital Status of the Potters

Marital status	Number of potters	Percentage
Married	103	85.83
Unmarried	17	14.17
Total	**120**	**100.00**

Source: Primary Data.

It is seen from Table 3.4 and Fig. 3.4 that, most of the potters 103 (85.83%) are married and remaining 14.17 per cent (17) of the potters are unmarried.

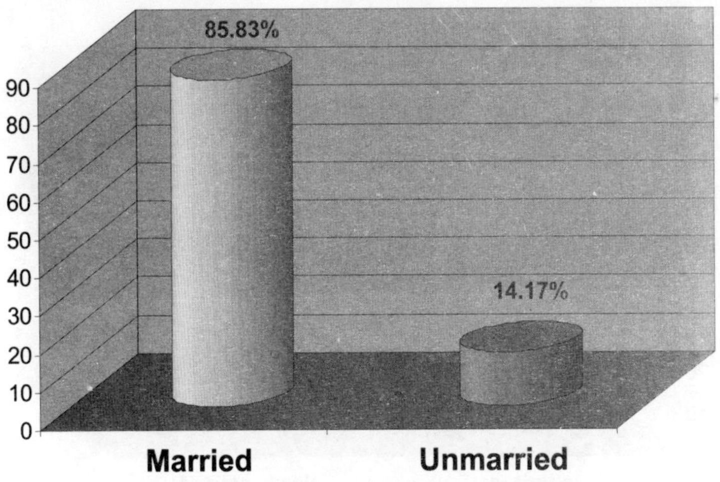

Fig. 3.4. Marital Status of the Potters

Nature of Occupation

Different kinds of occupation reflect the base of their socio-economic culture. The nature of occupation of the potters generally influences the working and living conditions of the potters. Pottery skills are learnt from their parents and grand parents as a continuity of tradition.[4] Table 3.5 and Fig. 3.5 represents the nature of occupation of the potters.

Table 3.5. Nature of Occupation

Nature of occupation	Number of potters	Percentage
Inherited	90	75
Newly started	30	25
Total	**120**	**100.00**

Source: Primary Data.

Table 3.5 and Fig. 3.5 indicate that, 75 per cent of the potters are inherited with the traditional pottery work. Only 25 percent of the potters have newly taken up pottery work for their sources of earnings.

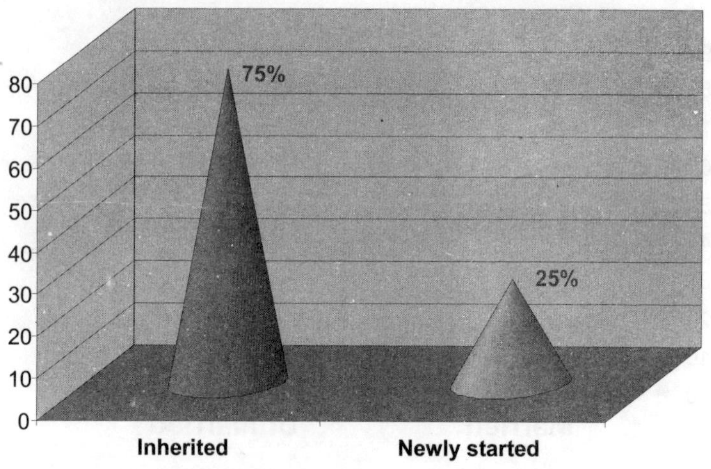

Fig. 3.5. Nature of Occupation

Traditional Occupation

Experience makes a person perfect. A person can make use of his experience while taking a decision and this minimises the

Table 3.6. Traditional occupation

Years	Number of potters	Percentage
Up to 20	26	28.89
20-40	29	32.22
40-60	31	34.44
Above 60	4	4.45
Total	**90**	**100.00**

Source: Primary Data.

chance of failure. Experienced persons improve their working condition by virtue of experience. Traditional occupation means those occupations that have been followed by successive generations of indigenous people and their communities and are rooted in customs and practices that were established prior to the colonization of the region in the nineteenth century. Table 3.6 and Fig. 3.6 shows the traditional occupation of the potters.

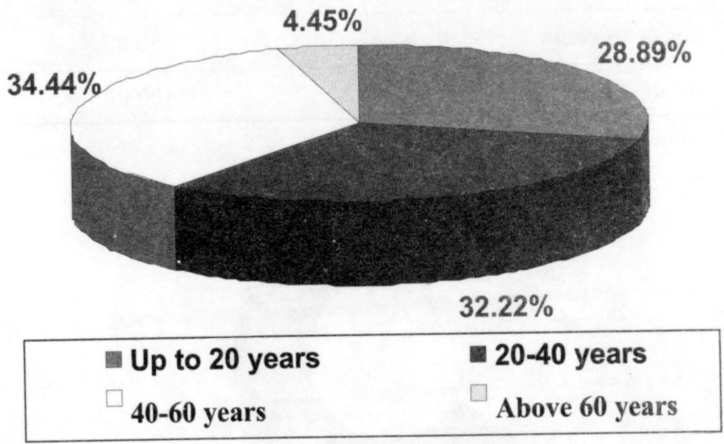

Fig. 3.6. Traditional Occupation

It is observed from Table 3.6 and Fig. 3.6 that, out of 90 potters who are traditionally involved in the pottery work, 31 (34.44%) potters have the traditional experience of 40-60 years. Nearly 29 (32.22%) potters are engaged between 20-40 years of experience and about 26 (28.89%) potters are between the experience of up to 20 years. Only 4 (4.44%) potters have the highest experience of above 60 years.

New Establishments

Rural women folk who come from agricultural backgrounds are capable of switching over to pottery after marriage as their husbands are traditional potters. Table 3.7 and Fig. 3.7 shows the experiences-wise classification of the potters

Table 3.7. Classification on the Basis of New Establishments

Experience of the potters	Number of potters	Percentage
Up to 5 years	12	40.00
5-10 years	8	26.67
10-15 years	7	23.33
Above 15 years	3	10.00
Total	**30**	**100.00**

Source: Primary Data

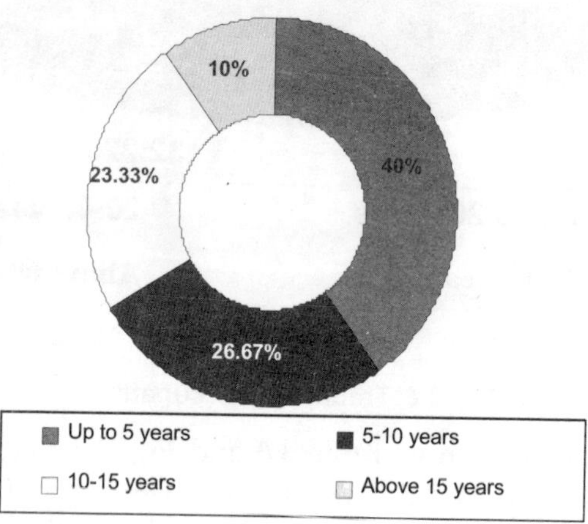

Fig. 3.7. Classification on the Basis of New Establishments

It is observed from Table 3.7 and Fig. 3.7 that 30 potters have newly started the pottery work. Out of them 12 (40%) potters have less than five years experience and 26.67 per cent of the potters have 5 to 10 years of experience. Only seven potters (23.33%) have 10-15 years of experience. Only 10 per cent of the potters have the highest experience of above 15 years.

Nature of Employment

Employment opportunity is the best parameter for the prosperity of the artisans. Depending on the nature of the business,the work may be on daily basis, seasonal and sometimes occasional. Table 3.8 and Fig. 3.8 represents the nature of employment of the potters.

Table 3.8. Nature of Employment

Employment	Number of potters	Percentage
Everyday	85	70.83
Seasonal	32	26.67
Occasional	3	2.50
Total	120	100.00

Sources: Primary Data.

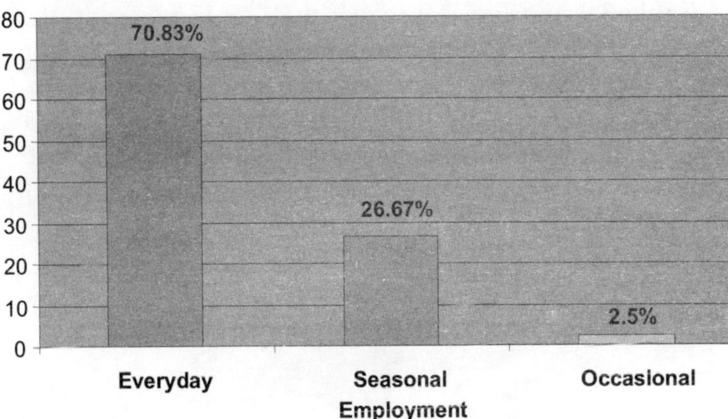

Fig. 3.8. Nature of Employment

It is evident from Table 3.8 and Fig. 3.8 that, 85 (70.83%) are engaged daily with the pottery work. Around 32 (26.67%) potters are seasonally involved with the pottery work. Due to non-availability of raw materials three potters (2.5%) are engaged occasionally with pottery work.

Earning Members

In the socio-economic analysis, the number of earning members in the family is considered to be an important factor for the prosperity of any households. Table 3.9 and Fig. 3.9 shows the earning member-wise classification of the potters.

Table 3.9. Classification on the Basis of Earning Members

Earning members	Number of potters	Percentage
One	34	28.33
Two	59	49.17
Three	11	9.17
Four	10	8.33
More than four	6	5
Total	**120**	**100.00**

Source: Primary Data.

Table 3.9 and Fig. 3.9 reveal that, 49.17 per cent of the potters have two earning members in their family, 28.33 per cent potters have only one earning member and other 11 (9.17%) potters have three earning members. Nearly 10 (8.33%) potters have four earning members. Only five per cent of them have more than four earning members in their families.

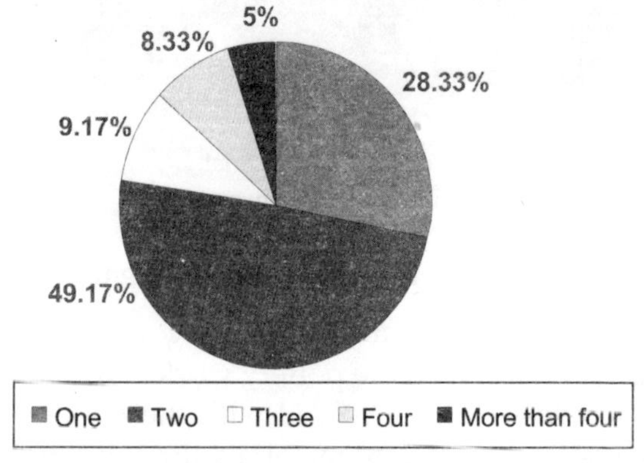

Fig. 3.9. Classification on the Basis of Earning Members

Earnings

Income is the consumption and savings opportunity gained by an entity within a specified time frame, which is generally expressed in monetary terms. Table 3.10 and Fig. 3.10 furnishes details about monthly earnings of the potters.

Table 3.10. Earnings of the potters

Monthly earnings Rs.	Number of potters	Percentage
Up to 1500	29	24.17
1500-3000	71	59.17
3000-4500	16	13.33
Above 4500	4	3.33
Total	**120**	**100.00**

Source: Primary Data.

It is evident from Table 3.10 and Fig. 3.10 that, 71 potters (59.17%) earn a monthly income between Rs. 1500 to (13.33%) 3000, 29 (24.17%) of them earn income below Rs 1500, other 16 potters earn between Rs 3000-4000.Only four (3.33%) of them earn above Rs. 4500.

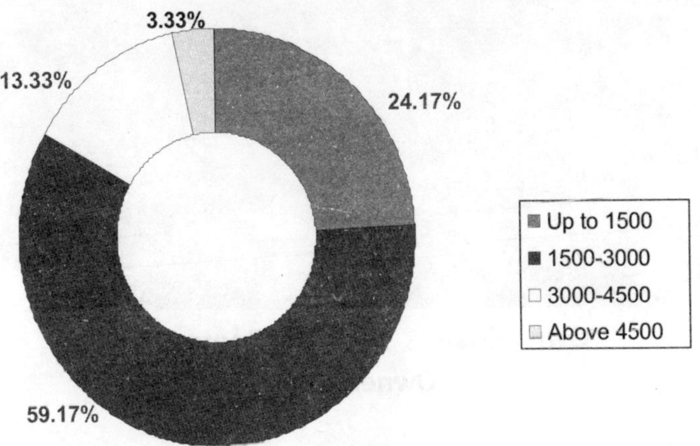

Fig. 3.10. Earnings of the Potters

Ownership of the House

Housing is a physical concept which determines the extent of civilization, sociological and economic advancement. The economic conditions of the potters are indicated by the ownership of their residence. Table 3.11 and Fig. 3.11 show the ownership of the house of the potters.

Table 3.11. Ownership of the House

Ownership	Number of potters	Percentage
Own house	88	73.33
Rented	32	26.67
Total	**120**	**100.00**

Source: Primary Data.

Table 3.11 and Fig. 3.11 reveal that 73.33 per cent of the potters are living in own house and 26.7 per cent of them are residing in rented houses.

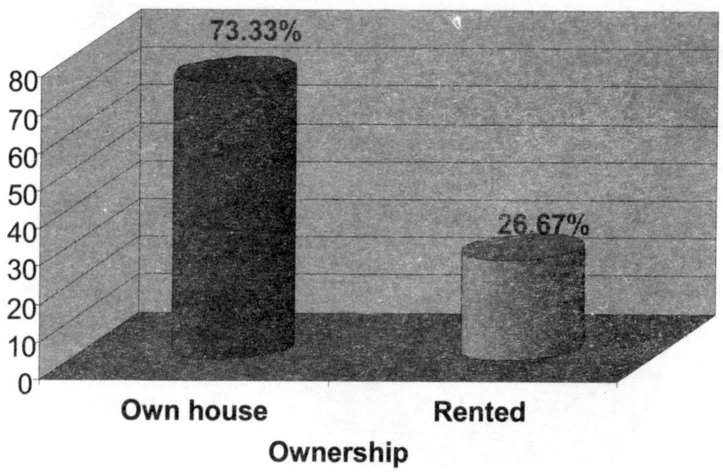

Fig. 3.11. Ownership of the House

Expenditure on Home Rent

Payment for the temporary use of a goods, services and property owned by some one else and the payment for such use are typically referred as rent. Table 3.12 and Fig. 3.12 shows the amount spent per month on rent.

Table 3.12. Expenditure on Home Rent

Expenditure Rs	Number of potters	Percentage
Less than Rs. 500	19	59.38
Rs. 500-1000	8	25.00
Above Rs. 1000	5	15.62
Total	**32**	**100.00**

Source: Primary Data.

It is inferred from Table 3.12 and Fig. 3.12 that, out of 32 potters residing in rented house, 19 (59.38 %) potters pay rent of less than Rs. 500. Between the rent of Rs 500 and 1000 there are 9 (25%) potters. Only five (15.62%) potters pay the rent of above Rs. 1,000.

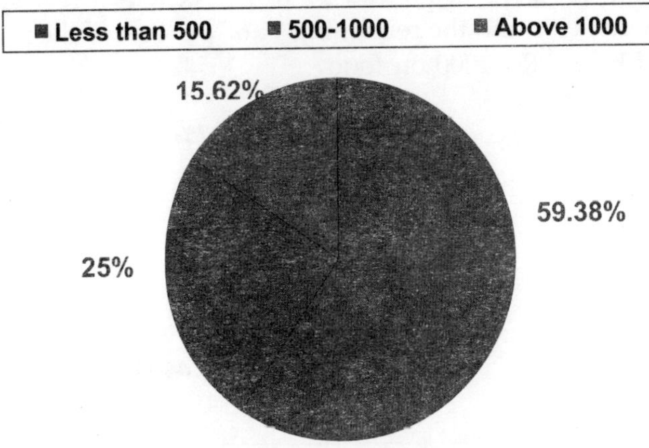

Fig. 3.12. Expenditure on Home Rent

Expenditure on Food Items

Potters in general, spend maximum of their earnings only for purchasing food items. The amount of money spent on food varies from one to another family based on their earnings. Table 3.13 and Fig. 3.13 shows the amount spent per month on food.

Table 3.13. Expenditure on Food Items

Expenditure on food Rs.	Number of potters	Percentage
Less than Rs. 1000	14	11.67
Rs. 1000-2000	53	44.17
Rs. 2000- 3000	30	25.00
Above Rs. 4000	23	19.16
Total	**120**	**100.00**

Source: Primary Data.

Table 3.13 and Fig. 3.13 show that, 53 (44.17%) potters spend between Rs. 1000-2000, 25 per cent of the potters spend between Rs. 2000-3000, and 19.16 per cent of them spend above Rs. 4000 and the remaining 11.67 per cent of the potters spend below Rs. 1000 on food.

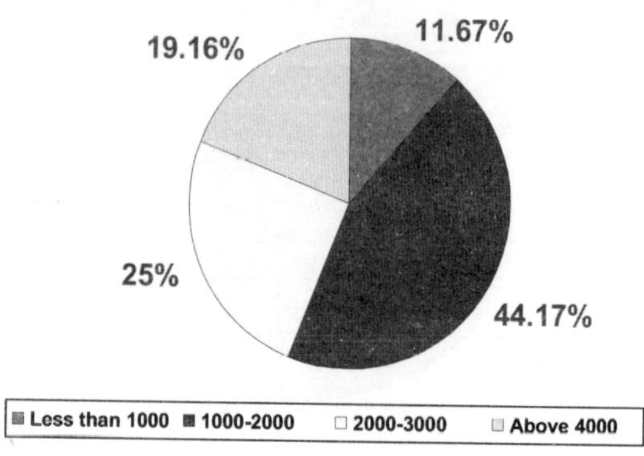

Fig. 3.13. Expenditure on Food Items

Expenditure on Education

The children of potters go to schools. The potters do not want their wards to take up pottery for making a living. Potters admit their children to government and aided school where the fee is paid back to them by way of scholarship. Table 3.14 and Fig. 3.14 show the amount spent for education per month

Table 3.14. Money Spent on Education

Expenditure on Education Rs.	Number of potters	Percentage
Less than Rs. 250	54	45.00
Rs. 250 - 500	32	26.67
Rs. 500 - 1000	13	10.83
Above Rs. 1000	21	17.5
Total	**120**	**100.00**

Source: Primary Data.

It is observed from Table 3.14 and Fig. 3.14 that, 54 (45%) of the potters spend less than Rs. 250 of their income for education of their children, 32 (26.67%) potters spend between Rs. 250-500. Nearly 21 (17.5%) per cent of them are able to spend above Rs. 1000. Only 13 (10.83%) of the potters spend between Rs. 500-1000.

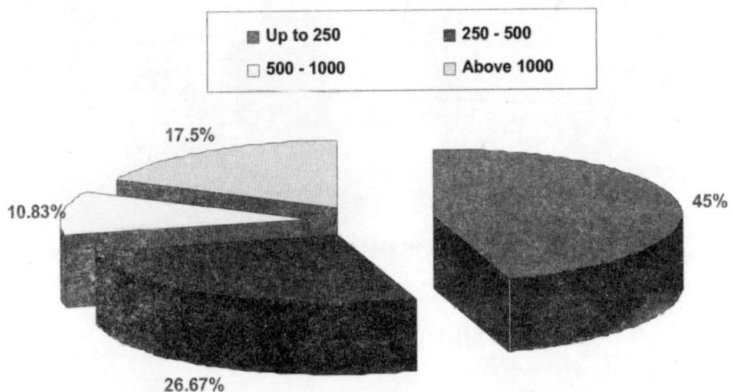

Fig. 3.14. Money Spent on Education

Nature of Hospital

A hospital is an institution for health care, providing treatment by specialized staff and equipment. Some of the potters get medical treatment from government hospitals, while others get treatment in private hospital. Table 3.15 and Fig. 3.15 represent the nature of hospital.

Table 3.15. Nature of Hospital

Nature of Hospital	Number of potters	Percentage
Government Hospital	82	68.33
Private Hospital	38	31.67
Total	**120**	**100.00**

Source: primary data.

From the table 3.15 and Fig. 3.15 it is revealed that 82 (68.33%) potters go to government hospital to take care of their health. Only 38 (31.67%) potters approach the private hospitals.

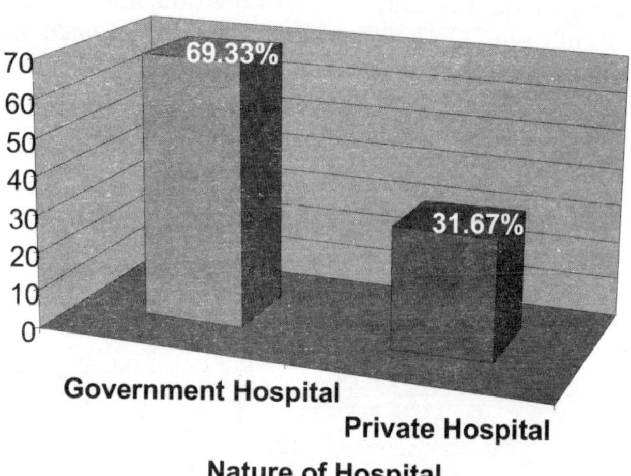

Fig. 3.15. Nature of Hospital

Expenditure for Health

Potters engaged in work with water and clay which leads to occupational diseases like head ache, cough, back pain. Only a negligible amount is spent by the potters for health care. Table 3.16 and Fig. 3.16 shows the amount spent for health care.

Table 3.16. Expenditure for Health

Expense per month Rs.	Number of potters	Percentage
Less than Rs. 500	28	73.68
Rs. 500-1000	8	21.05
Above Rs. 1000	2	5.27
Total	**38**	**100.00**

Source: primary data.

It is inferred from Table 3.16 and Fig. 3.16 that, majority of potters (73.68%) are spending below Rs. 500. 21.05 per cent moved to government hospital for their treatment and the rest 5.27 per cent of sample potters spend above Rs. 1000 for the health care.

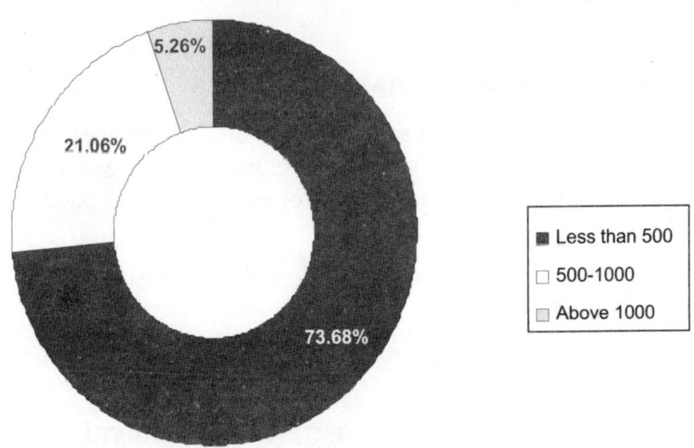

Fig. 3.16. Expenditure For Health

Savings

Savings is the excess of income over expenditure. The habit of saving of the potters is very low due to lower wages and high cost of living. The amount of savings varies depending on the earning capacity of the potters. Savings is considered to be one of the major determinants of economic development. Table 3.17 presents the details of the savings of the potters.

Table 3.17. Savings of the Potters

Savings	Number of potters	Percentage
Upto Rs. 250	62	51.67
Rs. 250-500	39	32.5
Rs. 500-1000	16	13.33
Above Rs. 1000	3	2.50
Total	**120**	**100.00**

Source: Primary Data.

From Table 3.17 it is inferred that, about 62 (51.67%) potters are having the habit of saving below Rs 250 per month, other 39(32.5 %) potters save between Rs250 and 500 per month. Only three (32.5%) of them save above Rs 1000 per month.

Multiple Regression Analysis

Multiple Regression analysis is used to analyse the relationship between, the dependent variable which is based on the independent variables such as age, educational qualification and income.

H_0 - Savings of the potters are not related to age, education and income.

H_a - Savings of the potters are related to age, education and income.

The formula for multiple regression equation is

$$\hat{Y} = a + b_1 x_1 + b_2 x_2$$

The result is presented in Table 3.18

Table 3.18

R	R Square R^2	Adjusted R Square	Std. Error of the estimate
1.000	1.000	1.000	

From Table 3.18 it is inferred that the adjusted R square (R^2) value is 1.000. It is seen that the independent variables age, educational qualification and income account for 100% relationship on the dependent variable, that is savings.

Mode of Savings

The mode of savings is different from one to another based on the amount of savings. Table 3.19 and Fig. 3.17 shows the different mode of savings.

Table 3.19. Mode of Savings

Mode of Savings	Number of potters	Percentage
Daily	13	10.83
Weekly	11	9.17
Monthly	96	80.00
Total	**120**	**100.00**

Source: Primary Data.

Fig. 3.17. Mode of Savings

Table 3.19 and Fig. 3.17 indicates that, for overall 80 per cent of the potters the form of savings is monthly. Nearly 13 (10.83%) potters do the savings on daily basis. Only 9.17 per cent of them have the mode of saving as weekly.

Sources of Savings

Savings is made by the poor, out of the economic use of money. Inspite of low rate of earnings, the potters show an interest in saving a part of their earnings for the future. Table 3.20 shows the sources of savings of the potters.

Table 3.20. Sources of Savings

Factors	Ranks					Total
	1	2	3	4	5	
Post office	13	34	40	25	8	120
Chit funds	11	35	28	26	20	120
Banks	45	10	23	29	13	120
Self interest	22	35	25	27	11	120
Financial institutions	29	6	4	13	68	120

Sources: Primary data.

H_0 – There is no significant relationship in ranks assigned by different potters regarding the source of savings

H_a – There is a significant relationship in ranks assigned by different potters regarding the source of savings

As there are four sets of ranking, the coefficient of concordance (W) for judging significant agreement in ranking by different respondents is worked out by using the formula,

$$W = \frac{S}{1/12k^2\left(N^3 - N\right)}$$

The calculated value of S = 10456

W = .074

To judge the significance of W the table value at five per cent level of significance is 112 and the calculated value is 10456. The calculated value is more than the table value. Hence the null hypothesis is rejected and it is inferred that there is a significant relationship in ranks assigned by different potters regarding the source of savings.

Indebtedness

Indebtedness is an economic problem of most of the potters. Low income, addiction to drink, lack of financial planning and social obligations contribute to high degree of indebtedness among the potters. Potters have to borrow money for their consumption expenditure. Table 3.21 and Fig. 3.18 show the debt of the potters.

Table 3.21. Indebtedness of Potters

Debt	Number of potters	Percentage
Yes	69	57.50
No	51	42.50
Total	**120**	**100.00**

Sources: Primary Data.

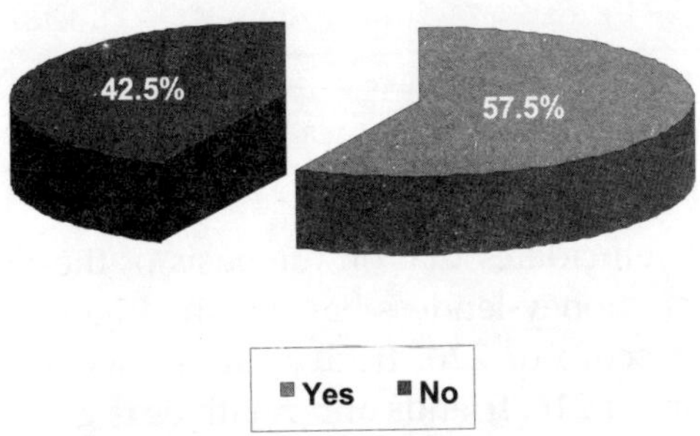

Fig. 3.18. Indebtedness of the Potters

Table 3.21 and Fig. 3.18 indicate that, overall 69 potters (57.5%) opined that they are having more debts and 51 (42.5%) of them do not owe any debts. During the off season the income from the pottery work is less and very few have other sources of income derived from livestock.

Sources of Borrowings

This study shows that most of the potter families are compelled to borrow money either for production or consumption purpose or both. Traders are those who attempt to generally buy whole sale and sell later at profit. Money lender offers small personal loans at high rate of interest. A bank is a financial intermediary that accepts deposits and lends loan. They also borrow from friends/relatives . The main reason for the increase in the indebtedness is lack of regular income during the lean season. Table 3.22 shows the sources of borrowings of the potters.

Table 3.22. Sources of borrowings

Sources	Ranks				Weighted Score	Weighted Average Score	Rank
	1	2	3	4			
Traders	33	20	8	8	216	1.80	II
Moneylenders	34	27	3	5	226	1.88	I
Bank	-	7	23	39	136	1.13	IV
Friends and relatives	2	15	35	17	140	1.16	III

Source: primary data.

Table 3.22 elucidates that on the basis of the ranks given by the potters, money-lenders has got the highest rank with the weighted score of 226, traders stand second with the weighted score of 216, friends and relatives is given the third rank with the weighted score of 140 and banks get fourth rank with the weighted score of 136.

Membership

Membership is the most important prerequisite for the development of the craftsman activity. Generally all the eligible potters enroll themselves as member of the craftsmanship in one of the available institutions. The function of the DIC is to develop and promote cottage and small scale industries in the district. The KVIC provides assistance to khadi and village industries which are characterised by low capital intensity and ideally suited to manufacturing utility goods by using locally available resources. The aim of the SIPPO is to develop entrepreneurship in rural areas and skill upgradation for rural artisans and the objective of the CAPART is to improve living conditions of the artisans in the rural areas, particularly the weaker section of the society. Table 3.23 shows membership of the potters.

Table 3.23. Membership

Membership	Number of potters	Percentage
DIC	30	25
KVIC	30	25
SIPPO	30	25
CAPART	30	25
Total	**120**	**100**

Sources: Primary Data.

It is observed from Table 3.23 that 25 per cent of the potters have been selected from each of the institutions like DIC, KVIC, SIPPO and CAPART.

Assistance from Government

A benefit through the government programme determines the growth of craftsmen sector to a greater extent. As a part of the development programme of KVIC, government has organised various programmes to train and improve the status of rural artisans. Improved tool kits and power tools are provided to improve the life of the potters. Subsidy is given to potters for construction of living cum workshed. Training is a major component for developing any member of workshops and skill development courses are conducted on a regular basis. Table 3.24 and Fig. 3.19 shows the assistance received through government programmes.

Table 3.24. Assistance from Government

Assistance	Number of potters	Percentage
Supply of tool kits	16	13.33
Loan/subsidy	35	29.17
Training	19	15.83
Power tools	50	41.67
Total	**120**	**100.00**

Sources: Primary Data.

Table 3.24 and Fig. 3.19 show that, the highest percentage of the potters (41.67%) are availing benefits from the government in the form of power tools, other 29.17 per cent are benefitted by getting the loan and subsidies. Nearly 15.83 per cent of the potters get training from the government. Only 13.33 per cent of the potters are getting tool kits facility.

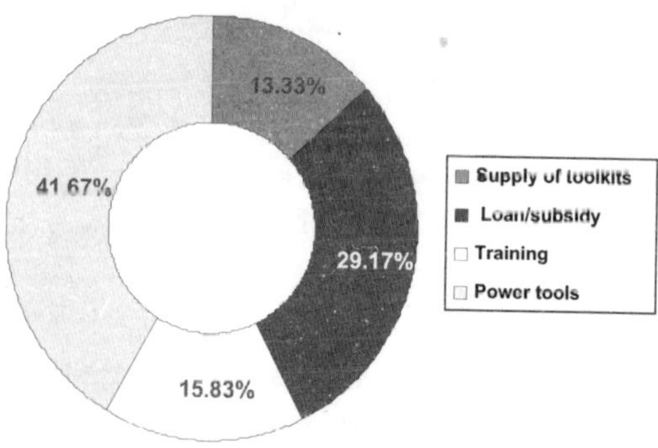

Fig. 3.19. Assistance from Government

Level of Satisfaction of Pottery Work

The levels of work satisfaction determine, to a large extent, the attitude towards work, management and trade unions. The level of satisfaction varies from one person to another. Table 3.24 gives details about the level of satisfaction of the potters.

Table 3.25. Age and Level of satisfaction

Age	Level of satisfaction			Total
	Fully satisfied	Some what satisfied	Dissati-sfied	
Less than 20 years	5	3	-	8
20years to 40 years	22	18	3	43
40years to 60 years	25	16	8	49
Above 60 years	9	8	3	20
Total	**61**	**45**	**14**	**120**

Source: primary data.

To test the difference in the single dependent variable satisfactions among the four groups formed by single independent variable, one way ANOVA is used.

H_0 - There is no significant difference between age and the level of satisfaction of the potters.

H_a - There is a significant difference between age and the level of satisfaction of the potters.

Table 3.25(a) show that the relationship between age and level of satisfaction of the potters.

As the calculated value (2.765) is less than the table value of F for $V_1 = 2$ and V_2=11at 5% level of significance (3.90), the null hypothesis is accepted. Thus it is inferred that, there is a no significant difference between age and level of satisfaction of the potters.

Table 3.25 (A). One Way ANOVA

Source of Variation	Sum of Square	V	Mean Square	F
Between groups	285.5	2	142.75	142F75 / 51.61
Within group	464.5	9	51.61	=2.765
Total	**750**	**11**		

Summary

The socio-economic status of the potters reveals that many of them have only primary education. It is also noted that the earnings are very low and their expenditure is more than earnings. In order to make good the deficit the potters borrow from other sources.

REFERENCES

1. Stephanson, *Economics of Labour in the Traditional Handicrafts Industries of Kerala*, p. 67.
2. Lalitha Bamba, *Techno socio-economic Survey of the Traditional Potter.*
3. Chandra Bose, *Socio-economic Condition of Workers of Firework Industry.*
4. Dogra Balram and Kharminder Ghuman, *Rural Marketing: Concepts And Practices,* Tata McGraw Hill Publications, p. 273.

CHAPTER

Problems of the Potters

Introduction

Working conditions refers to the physical environment under which employees have to work. It includes matters such as permitted breaks, the state of heating, lighting, and ventilation of workplaces, the safety and comfort of machinery, vehicles, and other equipment, normal manning levels, and disciplinary procedures.

The opinions of the potters are studied with regard to the influencing factors such as environment, finance problem, technology, occupation diseases, marketing and the inferior status of their occupation.

Factor Anlaysis

Factor analysis is a technique used in identifying a smaller number of factors underlying a large number of observed variables. Variables that have a high correlation between them, and are largely independent of other subsets of variables, are combined into factors.

Mathematically factor anlaysis is somewhat similar to multiple regression analysis in that each variable is expressed as a linear in that each variable is expressed as a linear combination of underlying factors. The amount of variance a variable shares with all other variables included in the analysis is referred to as communality. The co variation among the variables is described in terms of a small number of common factors plus a unique factor for each variable.

Table 4.1. The Initial Eigen Value

Component	Initial Eigen Value		
	Total	Percentage of Variance	Cumulative
1	3.547	23.644	23.644
2	1.729	11.528	35.172
3	1.521	10,137	45.309
4	1.255	8.363	53.672
5	1.138	7.584	61.256
6	1.020	6.797	68.053
7	0.955	6.368	74.421
8	0.712	4.748	79.169
9	0.709	4.728	83.897
10	0.576	3.838	87.735
11	0.483	3.221	90.944
12	0.448	2.987	93.944
13	0.381	2.541	96.485
14	0.310	2.066	98.551
15	0.217	1.449	100.000

The first stage in factor analysis is the factor called extraction process, where the objective is to identity how many factors will be extracted from the data and that is done by using principal components anlaysis. The extraction of factors depends upon the Eigen values. The higher the eigen value of the factor the higher is the amount of variance explained by the factors.

The second stage is the rotation of principal components that identifies which factors are associated with which of the original variables. The loading of each variable on each of the extracted factors is given by the rotated matrix value close to represent high loadings and those close 1 to 0 represents low loadings. The main objective of the study is to find out the variables which have a high loading on one factor but low loadings on other factors.

In this study the rotated sum of squared loadings indicated that six statements are enough to explain 68 per cent of the opinion. The eigen values are given in Table 4.1. The rotated sums of squared loadings are given in table 4.2

Table 4.2. Rotated Sums of Squared Loadings

Factors	Total	Percentage of Variance	Cumulative Percentage
1	2.300	15.336	15.336
2	1.928	12.852	28.188
3	1.846	12.308	40.496
4	1.450	9.666	50.162
5	1.409	9.391	59.553
6	1.275	8.501	68.053

The rotated factor matrix with communalities are given in Table 4.3.

Table 4.3. Rotated Factor Matrix

Variables	Factor I	Factor II	Factor III	Factor IV	Factor V	Factor VI	Commu-nalities
Inadequate work place	**0.820**						0.804
Heavy work load	**0.801**						0.770
Lack of storage facility	**0.572**						0.618
Non availability of raw material	**0.535**						0.809
Pollution from kiln is not controllable	**0.532**						0.588
Non availability of finance in time		**.758**					0.690
High interestrate		**.704**					0.699
Unaware of modernization			**.672**				0.538
No machine for preparation of clay			**.654**				0.476
Lack of technical guidance			**.633**				0.654
Lack of technology exposure			**.547**				0.551
Occupational diseases				**.829**			0.709
Less demand for the product					**.779**		0.716
Exploitation by intermediaries					**.720**		0.758
Inferior feeling about the status					**.908**		0.828

From the rotated factor matrix it is clear that four statements have come under factor I with high factor loadings. Table 4.4 shows the statements with high factor loading.

Table 4.4. Factor I—Statement with High Loadings

Statement	Factor Loadings
Inadequate work place	0.820
Heavy work load	0.801
Lack of storage facility	0.572
Non availability of raw material	0.535

All the variables are combined to a common factor called "environment". The working environment brings out the real situation of any trade or occupation. A good work environment facilitates production function and ultimately benefits the potters. The inadequate work place is one of the problems faced by potters. Raw material plays a vital role in the production of any trade and the potters are facing problems even in procuring the raw material. Due to rainy seasons, deforestation and restriction imposed from time to time by government, the collection of required quantities of raw material such as clay and firewood from local areas has become a difficult job. Adequate availability of raw material is a must for manufacturing and sustaining the rural industrial activities. The potters also face certain set back due to lack of proper storage facility. Potters carry out the work in their own house, which is mostly very small in size. When the raw material is collected in large quantity and production is in bulk, the house premises of the potters do not accommodate the entire quantity of stock.

The pollution from the clay preparation and from the pit which was replaced with an updraught kiln constructed in the courtyard of a potter is uncontrollable. It is interpreted that 82 per cent of the potters opine that they face problem related to work place.

From the rotated factor matrix it is shown that two statements have come under factor II with high factor loadings. Table 4.5 shows the statements with high factor loading.

Table 4.5. Factor II Statement with High Loadings

Statement	Factor Loadings
Non availability of finance in time	.758
High interest rate	.704

Both these variables are combined into a common factor called "finance". Due to lack of financial resources the potters are not able to buy raw material in bulk which makes their production cost high and profit lower. The potters are not provided with the necessary working capital during seasons time by the financial institution. During peak seasons, to have continuous flow of work, potters get finance from money lenders at high rate of interest. Being illiterate and ignorant the simple potters are not able to know that they are exploited by money lenders. It is interpreted that 75 per cent of the potters are facing the problem in getting finance in time.

From the rotated factor matrix it is evident that four statements have come under factor III with high factor loadings. Table 4.6 shows the statements with high factor loading.

Table 4.6. Factor III Statement with High Loadings

Statement	Factor Loadings
Unaware of modernization	.672
No machine for preparation of clay	.654
Lack of technical guidance	.633
Lack of technology exposure	.547

All the related variables are combined under one factor called "technology". Lack of know-how and skill on the part of the potters prevent them from adopting modern technology. The facilities for training the potters are also limited. Due to inadequate education, lack of interest and finance, the potters are not able take up training programmes.

Non availability of modern machines for mixing the clay for pot making also shows lack of technological upgradation. The rural artisans like potters are not exposed to latest technologies, as they live in a single room hutments which is also the workshop. Sixty seven per cent of the potters expressed that they are unaware of modernisation.

From the rotated factor matrix it is clear that one statement has come under factor IV with high factor loadings. Table 4.7 shows the statement with high factor loading.

Table 4.7. Factor IV Statement with High Loadings

Statement	Factor Loadings
Occupational Diseases	.829

The health problems reported from different craft segment are generally different from each other and depend on the nature of the work. Poor lighting, long working hours, poor work place, inadequate sanitation and lack of awareness of chemical risks which are multiplied by poor nutrition lead to certain occupational diseases. Potters suffer from occupational diseases such as back ache, swelling on the shoulder and eye problem that are caused due to long working hours, repetitive action of leaning over the wheel, carrying the finished goods on shoulder to long distance places for selling, Minute hand work affecting eye sight and watching the fire condition in the kiln causing breathing and eye problems. It is interpreted that 82 per cent of the potters suffer from occupational diseases.

From the rotated factor matrix two statements have come under factor V with high factor loadings. Table 4.8 shows the statements with high factor loading.

Table 4.8. Factor V Statement with High Loadings

Statement	Factor Loadings
Less demand for the product	.779
Exploitation by intermediaries	.720

All the related variables are combined under one factor called "marketing problems". Potters also face difficulties in marketing their products. The potters either market their products by self or through agents and middlemen, or through co-operative societies. Moreover, they expressed the view that customers are not paying a proper price for their product. There is also a complaint from the potters that there is less demand for their products. Decreasing natural resources, increasing demand for non-traditional products, high production cost and competition from synthetic articles are putting them out of their traditional work.

When the products are sold through middlemen and agents the prices received by potters are considerably much lower. The middlemen place orders on payment of certain percentage of money. At the time of collecting the products they do bargain and potters do not the remunerative price. 78 per cent of the potters opine that the demand for their product is less.

From the rotated factor matrix it is depicted that one statement has come under factor VI with high factor loadings. Table 4.9 shows the statement with high factor loading.

Table 4.9. Factor VI Statement with High Loadings

Statement	Factor Loadings
Inferior feeling about the status	.908

The social status of the potter is very low. Being illiterate and ignorant, the profession makes them feel inferior of themselves. Many potters live in unfurnished tiled houses, some of them live under their kiln roof and no separate shelter for living is available. The potters are uncomfortable with no electricity and toilet facilities also. The living conditions make them feel inferior. Ninety per cent of the potters have shown their inferior status of their profession.

Conclusion

The factors highlighted by the problem are the environment, finance problem, technology, occupation diseases, marketing and inferior status of their occupation.

Measures to Improve Pottery Business

Inspite of all the constraints, improvement can be brought in pottery business by making the raw material easily availabile, providing training, and product development through advertising and proper package. Measures to boost export are also essential.[1] Table 4.10 shows the measures to improve pottery business

Table 4.10. Measures to Improve Pottery Business

Measures for improvement	Ranks							Total
	1	2	3	4	5	6	7	
Easy availability of raw material	79	23	6	6	-	-	6	120
Reasonable price	11	35	40	27	6	1	-	120
Training on modern techniques	3	4	23	32	41	11	6	120
Establishing market linkage	10	23	24	21	24	11	7	120
Advertising	-	3	6	18	10	56	27	120
Package and storage facility	17	30	18	13	24	7	11	120
Exports possibility	-	2	3	3	15	34	63	120

Source: primary data.

The Garret's score is presented below in Table 4.10(a)

Analysis of the factors in Table 4.10 brings to light the rank order of the factors which bring remedial measures to improve pottery business. Easy availability of raw material is ranked first with Garretts' score of 8322, followed by reasonable price (Garrett's score of 7099). Package and storage facility occupies the third place with the Garrett's mean score of 53.85. The fourth rank goes to establishing the market linkage (Garrett's mean score of 51.25). The fifth rank for the training on modern techniques with the Garrett's mean score of 49.77 and advertisement occupies the sixth place with Garrett's mean score of 31.55 and export possibility was the last factor which brings the Garrett's mean score of 29.91

Table 4.10 (a). Garret's score

Measures for improvement	Garret's score	Average Score	Rank
Easy availability of raw material	8322	69.35	I
Reasonable price	7099	59.158	II
Training on modern techniques	5692	49.77	V
Establishing market linkage	6150	51.25	IV
Advertising package and storage facility	3787	31.55	VI
Package and storage facility	6462	53.85	III
Exports possibility	3589	29.91	VII

Willingness to Continue

Pottery is followed still by many potters as a traditional occupation. Some, as they do not know anything else to do, continue with pottery work. Those working in pottery units go to work as masons, or to work in brick-kilns also. The children of potters go to schools. Many of the potters have given up and moved away from their traditional occupation It was found that hardly anybody comes to take up pottery as an occupational proposition in recent years.[2] Table 4.11 shows the details regarding the willingness to continue the pottery work.

Table 4.11. Willingness to continue pottery work

Willingness	Number of potters	Percentage
Yes	93	77.5
No	27	22.5
Total	**120**	**100**

Source: Primary data.

From Table 4.11 it is inferred that 77.5 percentage of potters are willing to continue with the pottery work. Remaining 22.5 percent of the potters hesitate to continue the work because of poor earnings from this trade.

Willingness to Continue and Level of Satisfaction

Table 4.12. Willingness to Continue and Level of Satisfaction

Willingness to continue	Level of satisfaction			Total
	Fully satisfied	Some what satisfied	Dissati-sfied	
Yes	50	37	6	93
No	11	8	8	27
Total	**61**	**45**	**14**	**120**

Source: Primary data.

To analyse the relationship between the willingness to continue and level of satisfaction, the Chi-Square test χ^2 is applied by framing the hypotheses such as,

H_0 - There is no relationship between the willingness to continue and level of satisfaction of the potters.

H_a - There is a relationship between the willingness to continue and level of satisfaction of the potters.

The result of the Chi-Square test is presented below in the table 4.12(b)

Table 4.12 (b)

χ^2 calculated value	3.256	Degrees of freedom of significance	2	Table value @ 5 per cent level

Since the calculated value χ^2 (3.256) at 5 per cent level of significance (d.f. = 2) is less than the table value (7.38), the null hypothesis is accepted. Thus, it is inferred that, there is a no significant relationship between willingness to continue and level of satisfaction of the potters.

Reason for Continuing Pottery Work

Tradition has come out as a major reason to stick to the pottery work. Lack of any other option of livelihood and their own inability to undertake any other option forces them to continue the same. Table 4.13 shows the reasons for continuing pottery work.

Table 4.13. Reason for Continuing Pottery Work

Reasons	Ranks					Intensity value	Rank
	1	2	3	4	5		
Traditional occupation	42	28	5	7	11	362	I
Enhancing creativity	-	16	31	26	20	137	V
Flexibility in work	11	20	33	21	8	284	III
Non availability of other jobs	36	19	13	8	17	328	II
Freedom in decision making	4	10	11	31	37	165	IV

Source: primary data.

On the basis of the ranks given by the potters, traditional occupation is the foremost reason for motivating to continue the pottery work with the highest intensity value of 362. Non-availability of other job stands second with the intensity value of 328. Flexibility in work is the third reason with intensity value of 284. Freedom in decision making is also one of the reasons to continue the pottery work. Enhancing creativity is the reason scored by the potters with intensity value of 137.

Conclusion

The potters can survive in a competitive world only when they possess the capacity to diversify and modernize their skills in tune with present needs. The needs of the modern rural consumer are changing fast. Measures should be initiated to promote their products. What potters urgently require is a package of services which include raw material, new design, credit and general guidance.

REFERENCES

1. Shailesh Kumar Singh (2005) *Living on the Edge—An Appraisal of Livelihoods in Rural Jharkhand*, p. 47-49.
2. Jeebika, *Western Orissa Rural Livelihoods Project*, p. 10.

CHAPTER

Summary of Findings, Suggestions and Conclusions

Introduction

The artisans constitute the backbone of the rural economy engaged in traditional and cultural practices in the villages. Potters were probably the first engineers in the history of human civilisation, the first group to be withdrawn from food production and to be engaged in a full time profession. This was necessitated because the production of earthen vessels for cooking and storage was a specialized task needing a lot of skill and long training. The potter's wheel was a momentous invention, ranking along with the mastery over fire, as one of those which most influenced the course of human development. Yet, the traditional potters constitute some of the poorest sections of the society; in India. Hence, a study on socio-economic condition of potters was undertaken.

In the present study, an attempt is made to provide an analysis of socio economic condition of potters with regard to the following aspects:

- Nature of occupation.
- Sources of savings.
- Sources of borrowings.
- Opinion on the problems faced by potters.
- Remedial measures.

Findings

The findings of the data collected from 120 potters are presented in this chapter. They are:

- Majority of the potters (58.83%) accounted are male.
- Majority of the sample potters (40.83%) fall in the age group of 40-60 years.
- Majority of the potters (46.67%) have completed only primary education.
- Most of the potters (85.83%) are married.
- Around 75 per cent of the potters are inherited with the traditional pottery work.
- Out of 90, 31 (34.44%) potters have the traditional experience of 40-60 years.
- Many of the potters (28.33%) are having two earning members in their family.
- Many of the sample potters (59.17%) earn a monthly income between Rs. 1500 to 3000.
- Overall 80 per cent of the potters' form of savings is monthly.
- The major proportions of the potters (70.83%) are engaged daily with the pottery work.
- Majority of the potters (73.33%) are living in own houses.
- Nearly 32 potters reside in rented house and out of them 19 (59.38%) potters pay rent of less than Rs. 500.
- Many of the potters (44.17%) spend between Rs. 1000-2000 on food items.
- Around 45 percent of the potters spend less than Rs. 250 of their income for the purpose of their children's education.
- Out of 120, 82 (68.33%) potters go to government hospital to take care of their health. Only 38(31.67%) potters approach the private hospitals.

- Majority of potters (73.68%) spend below Rs 500 for their health care.
- Most of the potters 62 (51.67%) have the habit of saving below Rs 250 per month.
- Multiple Regression analysis is used to analyse the relationship between savings of the potters, the dependent variable which is based on the independent variables such as age, educational qualification and income. The result of adjusted R square (R^2) value is 1.000. It is seen that the independent variables age, educational qualification and income account for 100% relationship on the dependent variable, that is savings.
- To judge the significance of W the table value at 5% level of significance is 112 and the calculated value is 10456. The calculated value is more than the table value. Hence the null hypothesis is rejected and inferred that there is a significant relationship in ranks assigned by different potters regarding the source of savings
- Overall 69 sample potters opine that they are having more debts.
- On the basis of the weighted average score given by the potters for sources of borrowings, money lenders gets the highest score with the weighted score of 226.
- The potters who are registered with DIC, KIVC , SIPPO, CAPART are selected by giving equal chance to each institution.
- Majority of the potters (41.67%) are benefited by getting the power tools.
- To test the difference in the single dependent variable satisfactions among the four groups formed by single independent variable, one way ANOVA is used. The hypothesis is proved that there is a no significant difference between age and level of satisfaction of the potters.

- The application of factor analysis technique showed that environment, finance, technology, health problem, marketing problems, social status are the main factors related to problems faced by potters. Among the factors rotated under 'environment', is the highest loaded factor inadequate working place, under 'finance', the highest loaded factor is non availability of finance in time', under 'technology' ignorance of modernization, another factor loaded is occupational diseases, under 'marketing problem', the highest loaded factor is less demand for the product and inferior status about their occupation is the another factor.
- With regard to the remedial measures to improve pottery business, the garret's ranking results shows that easy availability of raw material gets the first rank with garret's score of 8322.
- While analysing the reasons associated with continuing pottery work, Traditional occupation gets the first rank with the intensity value of 632.
- To analyse the relationship between the willingness to continue and the level of satisfaction of the potters the Chi-square test is used. The hypothesis is proved that there is a no significant relationship between willingness to continue and level of satisfaction of the potters

Suggestions

On the basis of the findings the following suggestions are made:

- Availability of raw material at reasonable prices.
- Storage facility for finished goods made by potters should be provided to them. It will reduce the involvement of middlemen.

- New scientific methods should be introduced to reduce pollution from kiln.
- Adequate marketing facility through the arrangement of marketing union centres at the district and state level.
- State government should come forward to purchase the products of artisans or arrange some agencies for purchasing finished goods
- Possibility of export should be explored.
- Efforts to attract the younger generation mainly the youth to learn and practise the traditional arts and crafts.

Conclusion

On the hole the potters are not capable of meeting their basic needs. Government and NGOs should play major role to improve socio-economic condition of potters and particularly to reduce the poverty level. Due to economic constraints potters are not able to buy implements and raw materials, government and other agencies may take some necessary steps for buying implements and raw materials for pottery work. It is very important to start income generating activities to increase of season income. Socio-economic conditions are is sound .Hence; the potter community urgently require the package of service which includes training, new design, raw material, credit, marketing and the patronage of general public and government.

A STUDY ON SOCIO-ECONOMIC CONDITIONS OF WOMEN ENTREPRENEURS

—**Dr. T. Jeyanthi Vijayarani and *S. Maria Nisha M. Com., M. Phil.

CHAPTER

Introduction and Design of the Study

Introduction

Entrepreneurship has been acknowledged as one of the essential factors determining the growth and development of any country. Entrepreneurship development is essential for increasing production and productivity in the primary, secondary and tertiary sectors for harnessing and utilizing material and human resources, or solving problems of unemployment and under-employment for effecting equitable distribution of income and wealth for increasing the Gross National Product (GNP) and percapita income.[1]

Women as entrepreneurs are now successfully gaining importance in men's world because of their economic independence, combined with the challenge of doing something on the encouragements they get from the family members. Their involvement in business, their less aggressive nature, patience, humanity and gentleness, compared to those of men under similar conditions, enable women to be sound personnel managers both outside and inside homes.

Women entrepreneurs always display an innate capacity to calculate and shoulders risks, with a problem-solving approach, and have a very high degree of achievement motivation. Women also do not lag behind men in projecting a positive image of their talents and achievements. The other characteristic of women entrepreneurs can be listed as ability to think independently, fertile imagination creative ability and the easy adaptability to any change at home or elsewhere and the resilience to cope with setbacks.[2]

Women entrepreneurs in India have to cope with various socio-economic problems. Society's attitude and support are the major determinants of women's entrepreneurial success. The social and cultural roles played by women may place an additional burden on them. As a part of their social binding, women have to perform household duties and simultaneously operate as business owners. A woman entrepreneur is expected to perform the role of wife, mother, daughter, and daughter-in-law and business woman. Only few women are able to manage both home and business efficiently.

In the last few decades, in developing countries such as India central and state governments and non-governmental organizations have recognized that women should be in the middle of the road of economic development. By and large they have to confine themselves to home based or house attached entrepreneurial activities, petty business and very rarely tiny and cottage industries. Indian, women are still performing only their traditional roles in their houses and in agriculture, poultry, dairy, piggery bee keeping, goat rearing, petty shop keeping, pickle, papad and sauce making. But today non-traditional enterprises are easily managed by women and are conducted excellently by them as the decision makers.[3]

The hands that rock the cradle should be able to break the impediments that stand in their way to attain economic, social and spiritual fulfillment. Business and Entrepreneurship are the areas that challenge the wisdom and efficacy of ordinary women today and it is worthwhile to look into the nature, mode of functioning problems and prospects of these entrepreneurs to provide them with proper assistance and support.

Statement of the Problem

Women are becoming entrepreneurs at a faster rate as compared to men. At present women entrepreneurs comprise 10% of the total number of entrepreneurs in India. Women-owned businesses are highly increasing in the economies of all countries. The hidden entrepreneurial potentials of women have gradually been changing with the growing sensitivity to the role and economic status in the society. Skill, knowledge and adaptability in business are the main reasons for women to emerge into business ventures. Socio-cultural barriers are sometimes great barriers for succeeding in their business career. Many business women find it difficult to capture the market and make the product popular. They are not aware of the financial assistance provided by the institutions. Women entrepreneurship is the thrust area at present, as the government, banks and other agencies are ready to serve this sector in order to enhance self-employment opportunities and women empowerment. The present study of women entrepreneurs is undertaken with the view to understand the nature, the conditions under which they are functioning and the problems and challenges faced by them in the course of their entrepreneurial pursuits.

Review of Literature

Venkatapathy (1993) in his article "Entrepreneurship development among women" found that women with metropolitan urban background are most likely to participate in business and industry, while women with semi-urban background are less professional, have less exposure, awareness and interest in business related activities and generally lack educational background. Dwelling upon the usefulness of entrepreneurship and general management courses the author opined that it would be useful to incorporate entrepreneurial development as a co-curriculum programme in various academic programmes.

Klein (1995) in her paper on "Returning to work : Challenge for Women" stated that problems of compatibility between professional and private life are usually resolved to the detriment of women. It was also observed that with few exceptions, it is women who interrupt their career, when family obligations require such a choice. He concluded that their reintegration into active life poses problems but it is necessary not only as a basic human right but also for economic efficiency.[4]

D.Lalitha Rani (1996) in her study of 100 women entrepreneurs in manufacturing, trading and service in Visakhapatnam city of Andhra Pradesh, analysed the socio-economic background of women entrepreneurs. She opined that in service sector enterprises the level of education of women entrepreneurs is higher as compared to the level of those in trading sectors. In the manufacturing sectors, nearly half of them had technical education. The study concluded that majority of the women entrepreneurs in the service sector were employed prior to starting the enterprise.[5]

Tara S. Nair (1996) in her study 'Entrepreneurship training for Women in the Industrial Rural Sector: A Review of Approaches and Strategies' made an attempt to review the strategies and approaches followed in the country over the past four decades. It is revealed that development strategies targeted at women cannot hence be fitted coercively into conventional, one-dimensional and deterministic moulds like the anti-poverty paradigm that a typical state sponsored sectoral programme cannot take care of such a synergistic approach. It is emphasized that the 'over aggregative' and 'misleading' categories of income and class are to be rejected; and the importance of gender as crucial parameter not only in analytical exercises, but also in policies and programmes is to be recognized.[6]

Maitreya Dixit (1998) conducted a study on "Women and Achievement" to evaluate the economic participation. It was found that women make an important contribution to family income. The lower the socio-economic levels of the family, the greater the proportion of total income contributed by women. It was concluded that most Asian women prefer to work near the home, to avoid conflict between their roles as homemaker and wage earner.[7]

Moto Shige and Masayuki (1998) have made a study on the working and the development of 'putting-out system' in Japan. The study showed how rural labour force with a very low opportunity cost was capitalised by promoting rural entrepreneurship. The study exposed the alternative route of economic development in which there is movement of the modern production base into the rural sector, rather than migration of the rural labour force into the urban sector. The study supported a way of development in which widespread industrial activities could be organized in a decentralized manner by exploiting not only the physical labour but also the entrepreneurial ability of the rural people.[8]

Kranti Rans (1998) strongly recommended a centralized and properly co-ordinated institutionalised arrangement for extending technological backing and for the commercialisation of the benefits of Research and Development for the improvement of women entrepreneurs. The awareness and the use of consultancy facilities available in the country appear to be virtually negligible among the women entrepreneurs. It was highlighted that there is a need to popularize and adopt modern methods to disseminate the information about the technologies and consultancy facilities available for women entrepreneurs.[9]

K.P. Saraswathi Amma and Sudarsanan Pillai P. (2000) in their study on women entrepreneurs in garment industries in Kerala pointed out that all successful women entrepreneurs had strong family support and enjoyed personal freedom and majority of women have concentrated in urban areas. They emphasized the need for Entrepreneurial Development Programme for helping women in non-traditional, high-skill and male-dominated activities.[10]

Seenivasagalu R. (2001) who conducted a comparative study on 'Women Entrepreneurs and Executives - A Comparative Study in Chennai city revealed that women entrepreneurs were mainly motivated by education and previous experience. It is recommended that promotion of women entrepreneurs is a better solution for unemployment and involvement of women in economic activities.[11]

L. Rathakrishnan and B. Sellammalle (2001) in their study on "Micro-women entrepreneurs and socio-economic empowerment" have made an attempt to analyse the role of women in generating income through micro-entrepreneurial activity in the fishing community. They also aimed to bring relationship between women entrepreneurs and socio-economic empowerment of the community. It was observed that the micro-women entrepreneurs generate more income than the male owing to dynamism of the women in selling the captured fish in the open market. They added that the participation of women in uplifting socio-economic status of the family is of paramount significance. It was concluded in the study that certain significant changes have been noticed with respect to improvement in demographic and economic status of the family because of the dynamic women.[12]

Mathialagan, R. (2002) has conducted a socio-economic study on women entrepreneurs of Chennai city and stated that the socio-demographic and economic variables play a significant role in shifting the women folk into a new stream of life. It was highlighted that women entrepreneurs prefer to do business in service sector.[13]

C. Beena and Sushma B. (2003) made a study on "Women entrepreneurs managing petty business" by taking a sample of 30 women entrepreneurs of Andhra Pradesh. They found that women entrepreneurs were engaged in activities like selling vegetables, and flowers. It was noticed in the study that these women have migrated from villages where they were involved in farming. The study pinpointed that selling fruits, flowers and vegetables requires minimum technical skill, but requires high lungpower and laundry, selling snacks and tea are skill based and are determined by caste and tradition.[14]

S.K. Dhameja (2004) in the study of 175 women entrepreneurs from seven districts of North Western India study, examined the opportunities, performance, and problems of women-promoted enterprise. Analysis of socio-demographic profile of women entrepreneurs covered that the maximum number of respondents started their units after completing their education, marriage and in some cases after acquiring a few years of work experience also. The study concluded that their families belonged to business professional background, strengthening the belief that business family background facilitates one's entry into the entrepreneurial world.[15]

The North Western India Study (2004) analysed motivational and facilitating factors. The study revealed that push and pull factors operated in relation to the entry of respondents in business. A large number of younger women had high level of motivation not only by the desire to become economically independent, and do something creative, but also to achieve job satisfaction by accomplishing some challenging tasks, and to compete with others. The study highlighted the socio-personal problems faced by women entrepreneurs non co-operation from family members, male dominance, dual duties and limited liberty given to women.[16]

S. Rajanarayanan (2004) in his article titled "Support systems for the success of women entrepreneurs" stated that self-employment is the best employment and entrepreneurship is the most important mode of self-employment. In India women have remained a neglected section of work force. He has included in his article the details regarding the role of women, risk faced by women entrepreneurs, the essential prerequisites for successful women entrepreneurs and support systems to assist women entrepreneurs. The study advocates the idea that entrepreneurship development is possible through motivation training including specific programmes of entrepreneurship development for different sections of the society which in turn reduce the social and technological risks faced by rural women entrepreneurs.[17]

K. Kamalakannan (2005) in his article "The role of financial institutions in development of women entrepreneurs" stated that the development of entrepreneurship is a crucial factor for the industrial development of a country. In India, women constitute 48.2 percent of total population. Any sustainable change towards progress needs involvement of women. Many organizations both at central and state levels have come up to cater to the needs of potential women entrepreneurs. The article highlighted the role of financial institutions, commercial banks and non government organizations engaged in financing and promoting entrepreneurship among women.[18]

Anil Kumar (2005), conducted a study "Women entrepreneurs: Their profile and factors compelling business choice" of 120 women entrepreneurs engaged in small manufacturing enterprises in six districts. Hence, an attempt was made to determine the factors that compelled women to enter business ventures. The study revealed that women have started participating in economic activities not due to family compulsions but to achieve a goal in life by making a successful career, and secondary to make fruitful use of free time.[19]

Sujata Mukherjee (2006), in her study "What Motivates Women Entrepreneurs - Factors Influencing Their Motivation" takes up a sample of 125 women entrepreneurs in service, trading, and manufacturing sector in Mumbai and Pune districts of Maharashtra, referred to as Western Maharashtra study, and examines factors influencing the motivation of women entrepreneurs. The entrepreneurs selected were of low income strata. The study revealed that the decision to start a business could not be solely explained by the entrepreneurial psychological factors alone. It is likely to be based on a combination of personal, environmental and social factors, together with triggering events. The study concluded that the respondents were motivated to entrepreneurship primarily to satisfy their socio-economic needs.[20]

Moli P. Koshy and Mary Joseph (2007) in their study "Women Entrepreneurship in the small scale industrial units : A Study of Kerala" give a detailed description of the entrepreneurship and the Small Scale Industrial units, status of women in Kerala and also the number of organizations and programmes setup in the country for the development of women entrepreneurs and growth of women entrepreneurship in Kerala. The study concluded that the considerable increase in the number of women entrepreneurs is a result of the various support measures extended by the government to increase the level of women participation in entrepreneurship.[21]

Valsamma Antony (2007) conducted a study on "Women entrepreneurs in the Informal Sector – A Study" a view to understand the nature and conditions under which they are functioning and the problems and challenges faced by them in course of their entrepreneurial pursuits. She stated that the women entrepreneurs today are an emancipated lot, a force to rockon with and they are bound to succeed in the field of business with their intrinsic qualities of human relations, perseverance, cash management techniques and winning tactics.[22]

S. Mathivannan and M. Selvakumar (2008) in their study "A study on socio-economic background and status of women entrepreneurs in small scale industries in virudunger District" stated the main objective of the study as the analysis of socio-economic background and status of women entrepreneurs in small scale industries in Virudhunagar District. The study concludes that ultimately, women entrepreneurship must be recognized for what it is. Nationally, it has great importance for the country's future economic prosperity. Individually, business ownership provides women with independence they crave for and with economic and social satisfaction.[23]

A. Sankaran (2009) in his article "Trend and problems of rural women entrepreneurs in India" stated that the prime objective is to review and critically examine the problems faced by the rural women entrepreneurs in the present context and suggest remedial measures to help and promote rural women entrepreneurs. The study concludes that women are gentle, imaginative and they have independent thinking, creative ability, easy adaptability and ability to cope with setbacks. It was added that rural women entrepreneurial activities based on education, training, capacity building and management skills are to be provided. The study concluded that, encouragement programmes, special counseling centres and special symposiums, seminars and workshops provided a spillover effect for both rural entrepreneurs and the nation.[24]

Scope of the Study

The study highlights the status of women entrepreneurs and examines the motivational factors which influence the women to become an entrepreneur. It also looks at various problems encountered by women entrepreneurs.

Objective of the Study

1. To study the theoretical background of the women entrepreneurs.
2. To analyse the socio-economic conditions of the women entrepreneurs.
3. To examine the problems faced by women entrepreneurs
4. To give suggestions and conclusions based on findings.

Hypotheses

To give specific focus to the objectives, a few hypotheses have been drawn up and tested using appropriate statistical tools.

- There is no relationship between the type of the family and the nature of business of the respondents
- There is no relationship between the type of family and working hours of the respondents.
- There is no relationship between the nature of business and working hours of the respondents.
- The extent of marketability of a product is not positively related to its educational qualification and also related to its experience.
- There is no special significance in ranks assigned by different respondents regarding the problems in running the business.

Research Design and Methodology

Research Design

Exploratory research has been used for this study. It is meant to provide more information about the problem of developing working hypothesis from an operational point of view. In this study exploratory research is used to find out the various factors motivating women to become entrepreneurs and the problem faced by them in business.

Sampling Technique

The stratified random sampling method is adopted. The Chamber of commerce, District industries centre, Non Governmental Organization and Khadi and Village Industries Commission are considered as strata. From each strata, an equal number of 30 registered women entrepreneurs are selected.

Collection of Data

Data has been collected from the primary sources with an interview schedule from 120 respondents in Madurai city.

Framework of Analysis

Factor analysis, Chi-square test (χ^2), Garret's ranking technique, weighted average method, Intensity value, One-way ANOVA, Percentage analysis, bar diagram and pie diagram were used to anayse the data.

Chi-square Test

Chi-square test is a non-parametric test used for comparing a sample variance to a theoretical population variance. When the cell frequency is more than five the Chi-square test is applied.

$$\chi^2 = \frac{\Sigma(O-E)^2}{E}$$

O = Observed Frequency

E = Expected Frequency

$$E = \frac{\text{Row total} \times \text{Column total}}{\text{Grand total}}$$

$\mu = (c - 1)(r - 1)$

μ = Degrees of freedom

When the calculated value is less than the table value the null hypothesis is accepted.

Garret's Ranking Technique

The formula for using the Garret's Ranking Technique is,

$$\text{Percent portion} = \frac{100\left(R_{ij} - 0.5\right)}{N_{ij}}$$

R_{ij} = Rank given for the ith variables by the jth respondents.

N_{ij} = Number of variables ranked by the jth respondents.

By referring to the Garrett's table, the percentage position estimated is converted into scores. Thus for each factor, the scores of various respondents are added and the mean score is estimated. The means thus obtained for each of the attributes is arranged in a descending order. The attributes with the highest mean score is considered as the most important factors followed in order.

One–way ANOVA

Under the one-way ANOVA, only one factor is considered. Then it is observed that the reason for the said factor to be important is that several possible types of samples can occur within that factor. It is then determined if there are differences within that factor.

Analysis of Variance Table for One Way Anova

(There are k samples having in all n items)

Source of variation	Sum of Squares (SS)	Degrees of freedom (d.f)	Mean squares (MS) (This is ss divided by d.f.) and is estimation of variance to be used in F-ratio	F – ratio
Between samples or categories	$n_1\ (x1-x)^2 + \ldots + n_k\ (X_k - x)2$	(k – 1)	$\frac{\text{ss between}}{(k - 1)}$	$\frac{\text{Ms between}}{\text{Ms within}}$
With in samples or categories	$\Sigma(X_{ji} - X_1)^2 + \ldots + S(X_{ki} - X_K)^2$	(n – k)	$\frac{\text{ss within}}{(n - k)}$	
Total	$\Sigma(Xij - X)2$ i = 1,2,.... j = 1,2,....	(n – 1)		

Factor Analysis

Factor analysis is a general name denoting a class of procedures primarily used for data reduction and summarization of the factor may be represented as;

$$X_i = A_{i1}F_1 + A_{i2}F_2 + A_{i3}F_3 + \ldots + A_{im}F_m + V_iU_i$$

Where

X_i = ith standardized variable

A_{ij} = standardized mulitple regression çoefficient of variable I on common factor *i*.

E = common factor *j*

V_i = standardized regression coefficient of variable I on unique factor *i*.

U_i = the unique factor for variable *i*

m = number of common factors.

The unique factors are uncorrelated with each other and with the common factors. The common factors themselves can be expressed as linear combinations of the observed variables.

$$F_i = W_{i1}X_1 + W_{i2}X_2 + W_{i3}X_3 + \ldots + W_{ik}X_k$$

Where

F_i = estimate of ith factor.

W_i = weight or factor score coefficient

K = number of variables.

Weighted Average Method

Weighted Average Method is used to rank the sources of information. Five point rating scale is used and each scale has been given a score according to the importance starting from 5 to 1.

$$\text{Weighted Average} = X_w = \bar{X}_w = \frac{\Sigma WX}{\Sigma W}$$

Where X_w = Weighted Arithmetic mean

W = The weightage attached to variables

X = The variable value

Intensity Value

To study the source of borrowing of women entrepreneurs five reasons are framed and for each reason Likert's scaling technique has been used. The scores are given in the order of five, four, three, two and one, for Rank 1, 2, 3, 4 and 5 respectively for each reason. The intensity value was calculated as follows :

Intensity value: $[R_1{*}5 + R_2{*}4 + R_3{*}3 + R_4{*}2 + R_5{*}1]$

R = Represents the ranks.

Kendall's Coefficient of Concordance

Kendall is a non-parametric measure of relationship. It is used for determining the degree of association among several sets of ranking of N objects or individuals.

$$W = \frac{S}{1/12k^2\left(N^3 - N\right)}$$

where $$s = \Sigma\left(Rj - \bar{R}j\right)^2$$

k = No.of sets of rankings

N = Number of objects ranked;

$1/12k^2\,(N^3 - N)$ = Maximum possible sum of the squared deviations.

Multiple Regressions

When there are two or more independent variables, the equation describing relationship as the multiple regression equation. Multiple regression is taking only two or more independent variables and one dependent variable.

The formula for multiple regression equation is

$$\hat{Y} = a + b_1x_1 + b_2x_2$$

Percentage Analysis

Percentage analysis is a simple tool used by all. It is used to give the clear cut information about the analysis.

$$\text{Percentage} = \frac{\text{Individual respondent}}{\text{Total number of respondents}} \times 100$$

Operational Definitions

Entrepreneurship

Entrepreneurship is an attempt to create value through recognition of business opportunity, the management of risk-taking appropriate to the opportunity, and through the communicative and management skills to mobilize human, financial and material resources necessary to bring a project to fruition.

Entrepreneur

According to E.E. Hagen: "An entrepreneur is an economic man who tries to maximize his profits by innovation, involve problem solving and gets satisfaction from using his capabilities on attacking problem".

Women Entrepreneur

Women entrepreneurs may be defined as the women or a group of women who initiate, organize and operate a business enterprise.

According to the Government of India, a women entrepreneur is defined as "an enterprise owned and controlled by a woman and having a minimum financial interest of 51 per cent of the employment generated in the enterprise to women".

Limitation of the Study

The study is restricted to women entrepreneurs in Madurai district only.

Chapter Scheme

- The first chapter deals with the introduction, objectives, statement of the problem, review of literature, methodology, operational definition, frame work of analysis and limitation of the study.
- The theoretical background of women entrepreneurs is given in the second chapter.
- The factors motivating the women entrepreneurs are analysed in the third chapter.
- The fourth chapter deals with the problems faced by the women entrepreneurs.
- The fifth chapter deals with the summarisation of findings and suggestions.

REFERENCES

1. Antony, Valsamma (2007) women entrepreneurs on the upbeat: A study. Southern Economist March 1.
2. Kasthuri, V. Manickavasagam and Jayanthi P " Women entrepreneurs: An analysis. Southern Economist 2007, May 1.
3. Dhameja, S.K., *Women entrepreneurs*, pp. 34.
4. Klein (1995) *Returning to work : Challenge for Women,* I.L.O No.12 May 1.
5. Lalitharani D. (1996) Women Entrepreneurs - A Study of Viskhapatnam City, New Delhi.
6. Nair, Tara S., "Entrepreneurship Training for women in the Indian Rural Sector: A Review of Approach and Strategies", *The Journal of Entrepreneurship*, Vol. 5 (1), pp. 65-94,1996.
7. Dixit, Maitreya (1998), *Women and Achievement - Dynamics of participation* and partnership' Kanishka Publication, New Delhi.
8. Shige, Moto and Masayauki (1998), *Rural based development of commerce & industry*, pp. 47-67.
9. Rans, Kranti (1998), Edt. Modern working women and the development debate investing in women's work and development' Kanishka Publications, New Delhi.
10. Saraswathi Amma K.P. and Sudarsanan Pillai P. (2000), "A Study on women entrepreneurs in Garment Making Industries in Kerala-A profile", *Management Researcher*,Vol. VII, PP-5-8, Oct 2000-March 2001.

11. R.Seenivasagalu, (2001) "Women Entrepreneurs and Executives-A comparative study' Ph.D Thesis, Madras University, March.

12. L. Rathakrishnan and B. Sellammalle (2001) "Micro-women entrepreneurs and socio-economic empowerment" August 15.

13. Mathialagan, R. (2000), "Women Entrepreneurs in Tamil Nadu-A Socio-Economic study of selected women entrepreneurs at Chennai city," Ph.D Thesis, Madras University, March.

14. Beena, C.and Sushma B. (2003), "Women Entrepreneurs Managing petty business-A study from motivational perspectives", Southern Economics, Vol. 42, No. 2, pp. 5-8, May 15.

15. Dhameja, S.K., Women Entrepreneurs-oppertunities, Performance and Problems, New Delhi, Deep and Deep Publications.

16. North Western India Study (2004), Social Welfare, July-Aug, 2008.

17. Rajanarayanan, S. (2004) "Support Systems for the Success of Women Entrepreneurs", Journal of Kisan World, Dec. 14, pp. 17 & 18.

18. Kamalakannan, K. (2005) "The Role of Financial Institutions in Development of Women Entrepreneurs", Kurukshetra, April, pp. 10-13.

19. Kumar, Anil (2005) "Women entrepreneurs: Their profile and factor compelling business choice". *GITAM Journal of Management*. Vol. 3 (2), pp. 138-144.

20. Mukherjee, Sujata (2006) "What motivate women entrepreneurs-Factor influencing their motivation". *The ICFAI Journal of Entrepreneurship Development*, 3(4) Dec. pp. 7-20

21. Koshy, Moli P. and Mary Joseph (2007), Women entrepreneurs in the small scall Industrial units: A study of Kerala, *Southern Economics*, Vol. 39, No. 17-22, March 1, 07, pp. 19.

22. Antony, Valsamma (2007), Women Entrepreneurs in the informal sector-A study, Southern Economics, Vol. 45, No. 17-20, March 1, 07. pp. 11.

23. Mathivannan, S. and M.Selvakumar (2008), A Study on socio-economic background and status of women entrepreneurs in small scale industries in Verudunagar District. *Indian Journal of Marketing*, Vol. 38, No. 7-12, May 5, 2008, p. 35.

24. Sankaran, A. "Trend and Problems of Rural Women Entrepreneurs in India, *Southern Economics*, Vol. 48, No. 4, pp. 11.

CHAPTER

Women Entrepreneurs : An Overview

History of Entrepreneur

The history of entrepreneurship began relatively in the 1950s when people began forming new ideas for jobs or businesses as individuals. Once this step of forming an idea had been accomplished they would go about turning their idea into reality. This began to flourish in the economy and create competition among already well established companies. The development of entrepreneurship parallels to a great extent the development of the term itself. The word 'entrepreneur' is French Word and, literally translated, means 'between-taker' or 'go-between'.

In the middle ages, the term entrepreneur was used to describe both an actor and a person who managed large production projects, where this individual did not take any risks, but merely managed the projects using the resources provided, usually by the government of the country. A typical entrepreneur in the middle ages was the cleric the person in charge of great architectural works, such as castles and fortifications, public buildings, abbeys and cathedrals.

The reemergent connection of risk with entrepreneurship was developed in the 17th century, with an entrepreneur being a person who entered into a contractual arrangement with the government to perform a service or to supply stipulated products. Since the contract price was fixed, any resulting profits or losses were the entrepreneur's. Richard Cantillon, a noted economist and author in the 1700s, developed one of the early theories of the entrepreneur and is regarding by some as the founder of the term. He viewed the entrepreneur as a risk taker, observing that merchants, farmers, craftsmen and other sole proprietors "buy at a certain price and sell at an uncertain price, therefore operating at a risk.

In the 18th century, the person with capital was differentiated from the one who needed capital. In other words, the entrepreneur was distinguished from the capital provider. One reason for this differentiation was the industrialisation occurring throughout the world. Many of the inventions developed during this time were reactions to the changing world.

In the late 19th and early 20th centuries, entrepreneurs were frequently not distinguished from managers and were viewed mostly from an economic perspective. The entrepreneur organizes and operates an enterprise for personal gain. Entrepreneur fixes current prices for the materials consumed in the business, for the use of the personal services employed, and for the capital required. An entrepreneur contributes his own initiative, skill and ingenuity in planning, organizing and administering the enterprise. An entrepreneur also assumes the chance of loss and gain consequent to unforeseen and uncontrollable circumstances. The net residue of the annual receipts of the enterprise after all costs have been paid, he retains for himself.

In the middle of the 20th century, the notion of entrepreneur as an innovator was established. The function of the entrepreneur is to reform or revolutionize the pattern by exploiting an invention or, more generally, an untried technological method of producing a new commodity or producing an old one in a new way, opening a new source of supply of materials or a new outlets for products, by organizing a new industry. The concept of innovation and newness is an integral part of entrepreneurship. Indeed, innovation, the act of introducing something new, is one of the most difficult tasks for the entrepreneur. It takes not only the ability to create and conceptualize but also the ability to understand all the forces at work in the environment. The newness can consist of anything from a new product to a new distribution system to a method for developing a new organizational structure.

In the next millennium, Indian women would have to cross a major threshold and enter an unknown land. They will have to walk a path where none existed with a sense to discover. They will have to encounter and live with excitement and enthusiasm as well as threats, fears, anxieties and terror. It is the thrust in the self, of the resources to be generated, of the courage to journey forth in a new land; to live through the terrain's of uncharted land that the women of today will shape the new identity.

Entrepreneurship

Entrepreneurship is the attempt to create value through recognition of business opportunity, the management of risk-taking appropriate to the opportunity, and through the communicative and management skill to mobilize human, financial and material resources necessary to bring a project to fruition.

Entrepreneurship is the purposeful activity of an individual or a group of associated individuals undertaken to initiate maintain or aggrandise profit by production or distribution of economic goods and services.

Entrepreneurship refers to the functions performed by an entrepreneur in establishing an enterprise. Entrepreneurship is regarded as what an entrepreneur does. Entrepreneurship is a process involving various actions to be undertaken to establish an enterprise. Innovation and risk bearing are regarded as the two basic elements involved in entrepreneurial functions.

Entrepreneurship, like many other economic concepts, has long been debated. It has been used in various ways and in various senses. It is an elusive concept that cannot be defined precisely. The word 'entrepreneurship' has been derived from a French root which means 'to undertake'. Today, people call it by various names, e.g 'adventurism', 'risk taking', 'thrill seeking', 'innovating', etc.

The concept and its theory have evolved over more than two centuries. In classical economic theory, it was a shady concept. In the long run and under perfect competition the entrepreneur either disappeared or at least changed over into a sort of general manager. It is only in recent years that entrepreneurship and the role of entrepreneurs in the process of industrialization and economic development have been recognized in both developed and developing countries.

According to Higgins, "Entrepreneurship is meant the function of seeking investment and production opportunity, organizing an enterprise to undertake a new production process, raising capital, hiring labour, arranging the supply of raw materials, finding site, introducing a new technique and commodities, discovering new sources of raw materials and selecting top manager of day-to-day operations of the enterprise.

Entrepreneur

The word entrepreneur is derived from the French word, "Entreprendre" which means to 'undertake', i.e., the person who undertakes the risk of new enterprise. The word entrepreneur, therefore, first appeared in the French language in the beginning of the sixteenth century. The word was also applied to the leaders of military expedition. But it was Richard Cantilon, an Irishman, living in France who first used the term entrepreneur to refer to economic activities. According to

Cantilon: "An entrepreneur is a person who buys factor services at certain prices with a view to selling its products at uncertain prices". Thus, to Contilon, an entrepreneur is a bearer of risk which is non-insurable.

An entrepreneur is an economic leader who possesses the ability to recognize opportunities for the successful introduction of a new product, new source of supply, new technique of production and who assemblems the necessary resources and organizes them into a group concern.

Women Entrepreneurship

Women entrepreneurs may be defined as the women or a group of women who initiate, organize and operate a business enterprise. According to Schumpeter an entrepreneur is an innovating individual who introduces something new into the economy. However, such innovators are rarely found in the underdeveloped countries. The primary need in these countries is not innovators, but imitators or the humbler entrepreneurs capable of exploiting the hitherto existing possibilities on a small scale. The enterprise of these people may be small and unimpressive when judged by standards of the developed countries.[1] But the high propensity to imitate can set in motion the chain reaction which leads to cumulative progress. Thus, in the Indian context, an entrepreneur is more an adapter and imitator than a true innovator. Any women or group of women who innovate, imitates or adapts an economic activity may be called women entrepreneurs.

According to the Government of India, a woman entrepreneurship is defined as "an enterprise owned and controlled by a woman and having a minimum financial interest of 51 percent of the capital and giving at least 51 per cent of employment generated in the enterprise to women". Women entrepreneurs are opposing the condition of employing more than 50 per cent women workers. They point out that this condition is discriminatory. Enterprise set up by women should be provided with incentives and support on the basis of their ownership and management characteristic and not linked with employment of women.

Institution Assisting Women Entrepreneurs

District Industries Centres (DICs)

Governments both Central and State, have in the past taken a number of measures for the development of small and village industries, but the actual achievements have been far below the expectations. Also the focus of attention for industrial development was mainly on large cities and State capitals to the neglect of district areas. In addition, multiplicity of institutions getting involved in small industries development and complicated systems and procedures made the job of promoting the industrial units an uphill task for small entrepreneurs. Hence, it was felt necessary to establish a development agency which could provide all services and facilities to village and small industries under one roof. Accordingly, the DICs were established in May 1978 in order to cater to the needs of small units.

Each district has a DIC at its headquarters. The main responsibility of DIC is to act as the chief coordinator or multifunctional agency in respect of various Government departments and other agencies. The prospective small entrepreneurs would get all assistance from DIC for setting up and running an industry in rural areas. Up to 1991 about 422 DICs have been set up throughout the country. These DICs have assisted more them 1.5lakh units generating employment for more than 10.3 lakh persons. The metropolitan cities of Delhi, Mumbai, Kolkata and Chennai have been kept outside the purview of the DIC.

Functions of DIC

Identification of Entrepreneurs. DIC develops new entrepreneurs by conducting entrepreneurial motivation progorammes throughout the district especially in Panchayat Union Headquarters and small towns.

Selection of projects. DIC offers technical advice to new entrepreneurs for the selection of projects suitable to them.

Provisional registration under SSI. After the selection of projects, entrepreneurs are issued with provisional SSI Registration which is essential for obtaining assistance from the financial institutions.

Purchase of Fixed Assets. DIC sponsors the loan applications to THC. SIDCO and banks for the purchase of land and buildings and it sanctions margin money under Rural Industries Project Loan Scheme payable to other financial agencies for the purchase of plant and machinery.

Clearances from various Departments. DIC takes the initiative to get clearances from various departments and takes follow up measures to get speedy power connection.

Assistance to Raw Material Supplies. DIC makes necessary recommendations to the concerned raw materials and machinery wherever necessary.

Assistance to Village Artisans and Handicrafts. DIC arranges for the financial assistance with the lead bank or nationalized banks of the respective areas.

Interest-Free Sales Tax Loan. SSI units set up in rural areas can get IFST Loan up to a maximum limit of 8% of the total fixed assets from SIDCO. But the sanction order from the same is being issued by DIC. The DIC also recommends the SSI units to NSIC for registration for Government Purchase Programme.

Subsidy Schemes. DIC assists SSI units and rural artisans to get subsidies such as power subsidy, interest subsidy for engineers, subsidy under IRDP, etc., from various institutions.

Training Programmes. DIC gives training to rural entrepreneurs and also assists other units giving training to small entrepreneurs.

Self-employment for Unemployed Educated Youth. This scheme was introduced in 1983-84 for youths between 18 years and

25 years with SSLC. Technocrats and women are given preference.

District Industries Centres are supposed to provide pre-investment, investment and post-investment assistance to entrepreneurs under one roof. These centres have done commendable work in the promotion of small industries, development of entrepreneurship and generation of self-employment. But much is still desired to be done to make the DIC really one-window service. Steps should be taken to strengthen and suitably restructure the district industries centres for playing a leading role in district level industrial development.

Khadi and Village Induistries Commission (KVIC)

KVIC was established in 1953 with the primary objective of developing Khadi and Village Industries and improving rural employment opportunities. Its wide range of activities include training of artisans, extension of assistance for procurement of raw materials, marketing of tools, equipment and machinery to producers on concessional terms.[1]

The KVIC provides assistance to Khadi and village industries which are characterised by low capital intensity and ideally suited to manufacturing utility goods by using locally available resources. There are about 26 specified village industries such as processing of cereals and pulses, leather, cottage matches, Gur and carpentry and blacksmithy, gobargas, household alluminium utensils, etc.

KVIC's policies and programmes are executed through 30 State Khadi and Village Industries Boards, 2320 institutions registered under the Societies Registration Act, 1960 and about 30,600 Industrial Cooperative Societies Act. Activities involving pioneering types of work, such as developing new industries in hilly, backward and inaccessible areas are undertaken by KVIC directly.[2]

Non-governmental Oraganisation

Women's nonprofit organizations have long played an important role in the lives of women in many parts of the world. In India, well-educated and affluent women find socially sanctioned work outside the home in the voluntary sector. They work as volunteers under the aegis of religious organizations and for social service nonprofit organisations dedicated to the alleviation of poverty. Participation in nonprofit undertakings in India gives women an opportunity to enter the social and political spheres in ways often denied to them by the for-profit and public sectors. Important changes in women's lives are a direct result of the intervention of nongovernmental organizations (NGOs). Many NGOs that deal with the alleviation of poverty for women often also focus on advocacy for women's rights as well as providing services for women

Chamber of Commerce

The Chamber of Commerce a professional affiliation of local businesses, is often associated with other civic organizations such as the Visitors and Tourism Bureau. Membership in a Chamber of Commerce is generally voluntary, although most local businesses do find strength in numbers. The main function of a Chamber of Commerce is to promote interest in local business possibilities.

A Chamber of Commerce also works within the community as a leader of civic projects. Sponsorship of local beautification programmes is often provided by the local Chamber of Commerce as a means to improve the city's appeal. The local government often turns to the Chamber of Commerce first when seeking the opinion of the business community. Membership in a Chamber of Commerce is generally viewed as a powerful endorsement by prominent local business leaders.

Chamber of commerce is one of various voluntary organizations of business firms, public officials, professional people, and public-spirited citizens whose primary interest is in publicizing, promoting, and developing commercial and industrial opportunities in their local area, and usually also community schools, streets, housing, and public works.

Functions and Role of Women Entrepreneurs

Women entrepreneur must perform five functions:

1. Exploring the prospects of starting new enterprises.
2. Undertaking of risks and handling of economic uncertainties.
3. Introduction of innovations
4. coordination, administration and control
5. routine supervision

All these functions appear to be somewhat uneven in character. Moreover, these functions are not always of equal importance. For instance, risk taking and innovation are paramount for establishing or diversifying an enterprise. Coordination and supervision become increasingly important in improving the efficiency and assuming smooth, balanced operation of the undertaking. In women enterprises, usually the same lady performs all theses functions; most likely, she is also the owner of the enterprise.

Women entrepreneurs can more easily undertake three types of industrial. enterprises: (1) operate purely as a sub-contractor on raw materials provided by the customer; (2) manufacture an item to the long or short term order of another enterprise usually a large scale unit; and (3) manufacture the item for direct sale in the market. Generally, the first two types of enterprises are known as ancillaries.

Women entrepreneurs produce both consumer goods and intermediate goods which are used in the production of other articles.

Growth of Women Enterepreneurship

In recent years women have made their mark in different

walks of life and are competing successfully with men despite the social, psychological and economic barriers. This has been possible due to education, political awakening, urbanization, legal safeguards social reforms, etc. Some of the women have distinguished themselves in many unconventional fields as prime ministers, ambassadors, governors, space scientists, pilots, vice-chancellors, administrators and entrepreneurs.

In business the entry of women is a relatively new phenomenon. On account of the break-up of the joint family system and the need for additional income to maintain living standards in the context of inflation, women began to enter the competitive world of business. A woman may start her own business due to several reasons. She may not be able to find jobs in the market place or she may not be able to work outside her house. Some women may start their own businesses as they are stagnating near the top of male-owned firms.

In India, women entrepreneurs constitute a negligible proportion of the total entrepreneurs. Attitudinal constrains, social traditions and kinship system inhibit the emergence of women entrepreneurs." The typical women enterprises are the extension of kitchen activities, i.e., the 3ps, viz., pickles, powder (*massala*) and papped, or the traditional cottage industries of basket making, etc.' in India women have contributed mainly in household industries due to the less technical know-how required and little competition from men in these industries. With the spread of education and the growing awareness among women, women entrepreneurs have entered into engineering, electronics, energy and many other industries. Although the number of such units is small, women are putting up units to manufacture solar cookers. T.V. capacitors, electronic ancillaries and small foundaries. Various government agencies and voluntary bodies, like mahila mandals, have accelerated the growth of women entrepreneurs in the country. Over the years, women have become more achievement-oriented, career-minded and economically independent. They want to widen their sphere of work and enjoy achievement.

Factors Determining Growth of Entrepreneueship

Entrepreneurship is the outcome of the interaction between several social, demographic, economic and political variable. These variables may be classified as follows:

Personal Characteristics

Personal characters consist of age, marital status, caste and religion, education and technical qualifications, etc. Personality and personal skill are very important. Age factor of new entrepreneurs is very significant in a developing economy. It acts as a critical factor in self development and growth of the organization. Young persons tend to be more optimistic in facing the challenges of life. Being exposed to the latest developments in science and technology, they are expected to be more innovative. Their outlook is less conservative and therefore they can bring greater dynamism in enterprise. Marital status may be conducive to entrepreneurial growth. In the cause of fulfilling family responsibilities one may be willing to face the challenges of entrepreneurship. Education and technical knowledge help to make an individual a more competent organizer and coordinator of resources. According to Harris, "perception of opportunities, gaining control over resources and managing in going enterprises are primary functions of entrepreneurship, regardless of the individual's willingness to undertake entrepreneurial activities. These desires will not be realised if the necessary capacity to carry them is lacking. Education, occupational experiences and access to technical information should each play a crucial role."

Education, though, not a deciding factor, influences the efficiency and success of entrepreneurs. Risk bearing and innovation require command over technology and an exposure to outside world. Education provides these and thereby improves the competitive strength. It also serves as contact factor to the new entrepreneurs without much social base and resources. Personal experience also contributes to efficiency in entrepreneurship.

Family Background

Family background plays a significant role in the growth of entrepreneurship. People belonging to merchantile families and communities can more easily enter industry.

Political Support

Official and social contacts are necessary requirements for success in business. Contacts at higher social and Government levels enable an individual in obtaining necessary approvals and institutional assistance quickly. In order to build up such contacts it is necessary to work with prestigious group individually or through relatives, friends and associations. Political affiliation social participation and such other linkages serve as an important factor contributing to entrepreneurship.

Economic Factors

Since entrepreneurship is essentially the promotion of economic change, the same factors that promote economic growth and development account for the emergence of entrepreneurship. Market incentives, available capital, and financial institutions that provide capital to entrepreneurial projects help to promote entrepreneurship.

Socio-cultural Factors

In countries like the United States, entrepreneurs and entrepreneurial behaviour enjoy a legitimacy they do not have in the Soviet Union. Political and economic ideologies and legal structure in some countries encourage free enterprise and protect the rights of individuals. Another factor that affects entrepreneurship is social mobility.

Women Entrepreneurs in Small Scale Industry

The position of women and their status in any society is an index of its civilization. Women are to be considered as equal partners in the process of development. But, because of centuries of exploitation and subjugation, Indian women have remained at the receiving end. Women in India have been the neglected lot. They have not been actively involved in the mainstream of development even though they represent equal proportion of the population and labour force. Primarily women are the means of survival of their families, but are generally unrecognized and undervalued, being placed at the bottom of the pile.

Women as an independent target group, account for 495.74 million and represent 48.3% of the country's population, as per the 2001 census. No country can achieve its potential without adequately investing in and developing the capabilities of women. In the interest of long-term development it is necessary to facilitate their empowerment. In many developing countries, including India, women have much less access to education, jobs, income and power than men. Even after five and half decades of planned development Indian women have not achieved expected success in the mainstream of life. Our country will be unable to have a competitive edge over others until and unless the status and role of women is improved.

Women are almost one half of the world's population having enormous potential but being underutilized or unutilized for the economic development of the nation. There is need to strengthen and streamline the role of women in the development of various sectors by harnessing their power towards nation building and accelerated economic growth.

Majority of women do not undertake entrepreneurial ventures. Entrepreneurship is a key to economic development of a country. History is full of instances of individual entrepreneurs whose creativity had led to the industrialization of many nations. Small Scale Industries (SSI) play a key role in the industrialization of the country. It is considered as an important means for checking concentration of economic power in the few hands and bringing about economic dispersal and more equitable distribution of national income. The nature and characters of SSI are suitable to women to become entrepreneurs. In this article an attempt has been made to view the participation of women entrepreneurs in Small Scale Industries.

Women Entrepreneurship in India

Table 2.1

States	No of Units Registered	No. of Women Entrepre-neurs	Percentage
Tamil Nadu	9618	2930	30.36
Uttar Pradesh	7980	3180	39.84
Kerala	5487	2135	38.91
Punjab	4791	1618	33.77
Maharashtra	4339	1394	32.12
Gujarat	3872	1538	39.72
Karnataka	3822	1026	26.84
Madhya Pradesh	2967	842	28.38
Other States & UTS	14576	4185	28.71
Total	**57,452**	**18,848**	**32.82**

Characteristics of Women Entrepreneurs in Practice In India

First category

- Established in big cities.

- Having higher level technical and professional qualifications.
- Non traditional Items
- Sound financial positions

Second category

- Established in cities and towns
- Having sufficient education
- Both traditional and non traditional items
- Undertaking women services kindergarten, crèches, beauty parlors, health clinic etc.

Third category

- Illiterate women
- Financially weak
- Involved in family business such as agriculture, horticulture, animal husbandry, dairy, fisheries, agro forestry, handloom, power loom etc.

Problem faced by Women Entrepreneurs

Women entrepreneurs encounter many problems in their efforts to develop the enterprises they have established. The main problems faced by the women entrepreneurs may be analyzed as follows.

Shortage of Finance

Women and small entrepreneurs always suffer from inadequate financial resources and working capital. They are lacking access to external funds due to absence of tangible security and credit in the market. Women do not generally have property in their names. Owing to the lack of confidence in women's ability, male members in the family do not like to risk their capital in ventures run by women. The complicated procedure of bank loans, the inordinate delay in obtaining the loans and the running about involved, deter many women from venturing. Women entrepreneurs also face the problem of obtaining working capital for financing day-to-day operations of their enterprises. Banks discourage women borrowers believing that they will leave their business and become housewives again. Women entrepreneurs rely often on personal savings and loans from family friends. Most of the women enterprises fail due to lack of financing.

Inefficient Arrangements for Marketing and Sale

For marketing their products, women entrepreneurs are often at the mercy of the middlemen who pocket large chunk of profit. Although the middlemen exploit the women entrepreneurs, the elimination of middlemen is difficult because it involves a lot of running about. Further, women entrepreneurs find it difficult to capture the market and make their products popular. This problem is all the more serious in the case of food production and processing ventures.

Shortage of Raw Materials

Women entrepreneurs find it difficult to procure raw materials and other necessary inputs. The failure of many women cooperatives in 1971 such as those engaged in basket making was mainly due to the inadequate availability of forest- based raw materials. The prices of many raw materials are quite high.

Stiff Competition

Many of the women enterprises have imperfect organizational setup. They have to face severe competition from organized industries and male entrepreneurs.

High Cost of Production

Another problem, which undermines the efficiency and restricts the development of women enterprise, is the high cost of production. Government assistance in the form of grants and subsidies to some extent enables them to tide over this difficulty.

Low Mobility

One of the biggest handicaps for women entrepreneurs is mobility or travelling from place to place. Women on their own find it difficult to get accommodation in smaller towns. A single women asking for a room is still looked upon with suspicion. Some of the woman entrepreneurs complain that government clerks and private dealers harass them as women are believed to be less able to go through complicated court proceedings.

Family Responsibilities

In India, it is mainly a woman's duty to look after the children and other members of the family. Her involvement in family leaves little energy and time for business. Married women entrepreneurs have to make a fine balance between business and home. Their success in this regard also depends upon the support of the husband and family. Without the support and approval of the husband, the female entrepreneurs cannot succeed. There arises a role conflict in many women entrepreneurs. Such conflict prevents them from taking prompt decisions in business.

Social Attitudes

The biggest problem of a woman entrepreneur is the social attitude and the constraints in which she has to live and work. Despite constitutional equality, there is discrimination against women. In a tradition-bound society, women suffer from male reservations about a woman's role and capacity. In rural areas, women face resistance not only from males but also from elderly females who have accepted inequality. The overbearing presence of elders restrains the young girls from venturing out. Rural women have the potential but they are not properly trained. It is believed that skill imparted to a girl is low when she gets married. Therefore, girls continue to be helpers in agriculture and handicrafts and do not become entrepreneurs. In a male-dominated society, women do not get equal treatment and male ego puts barriers in their progress.

Low Ability to Bear Risk

Women have comparatively a low ability to bear economic and other risks because they have led a protected life. Sometimes they face discrimination in the selection for entrepreneurial development training. Some of them lack entrepreneurial initiative or specialized training. Inferiority complex, unplanned growth, lack of infrastructure, and late start are other problems of women entrepreneurs in India.

Lack of Education

In India literacy among women is very low. Due to lack of education, majority of women are unaware of technological developments, marketing knowledge, etc. Lack of information and experience creates further problems in the setting up and running of business enterprises.

Remedies to Solve the Problems of Women Entrepreneurs

Finance Cells

In various public financial institutions and banks special cells may be opened for providing easy finance to women entrepreneurs. These cells should be made to provide finance at the local level. Finance to women entrepreneurs may be provided at concessional rates of interest and on easy repayment basis.

Marketing Cooperative

Encouragements and assistance should be provided to women entrepreneurs for setting up cooperatives. These cooperatives will pool the inputs of women enterprises and sell them on remunerative prices. Such cooperatives will help to eliminate the middlemen. Central and State Governments should give priority to women entrepreneurs while purchasing for their requirement.

Supply of Rawmaterials

Scarce and imported raw materials may be made available to women entrepreneurs on priority basis. A subsidy may also be given to make the products manufactured by women entrepreneurs.

Education and Awareness

It is necessary to change negative social attitudes towards women. Elders, particularly, mothers and mothers -in-law, need to be made aware of the potential of girls and their due role in society. Unless the social attitudes are made positive not much progress can be made by women entrepreneurs.

Training Facilities

Training and skills are essential for the development of entrepreneurship. Training schemes should be so designed that women can take full advantage of them. Family members do not like women to go away to far off places for training. Therefore, mobile training centres should be arranged.[3] Similarly, part time training facilities, especially during afternoons will attract more women to acquire skills. Additional facilities like stipend, good hygienic crèches, transport facilities, etc., should be offered to attract more and more women to the training centres.

Women have the potential and the will to establish and manage enterprise of their own. What they need is encouragement and support. Government and public enterprises should offer ancillary units to women entrepreneurs on priority basis. With the assistance of family members and the government women can join the main stream of national economy and thereby, contribute to the country's economic progress.

Conclusion

Women entrepreneurs have become a strong driving force in today's corporate world. They are able to balance their duties of both motherhood and entrepreneurship. They also comprise of almost half of all business enterprises today.

REFERENCES

1. Women entrepreneurship in India, *Southern Economists*, Vol. 38, No. 1-4 , June 15, 1999, pp. 11.
2. Gupta.C.B and Dr.Srinivasan.N.P., *Entrepreneurship* development in India, Sultan Chand & Sons.

CHAPTER

Socio-Economic Conditions of Women Enterprises

Introduction

Women development has been considered vital for the overall sustainable development of the nation. The necessity of development of women has been realized today. Women's empowerment and their full participation on the basis of equality in all spheres of society are fundamental for the achievement of equity, development and peace. Upliftment of women is an essential ingredient of human progress. Entrepreneurship development among the women force will strengthen the economy and promote regional development.[1]

The challenges and opportunities provided to the women of digital era are growing so rapidly that the job seekers are turning into job creators. They are flourishing as designers, interior decorators, exporters, publishers, garment manufacturers and are found exploring new avenues of economic participation. In India, though women constitute nearly half of the total population, the entrepreneurial world is still a male dominated one. Women in advanced nations are recognized and are more prominent in the business world.[2]

In this chapter an attempt is made to study and analyse the,

- Profile of the women entrepreneurs
- Experience of the women entrepreneurs
- Sources of information

- Sources of borrowings
- Opinion on entrepreneurs

Age of the Respondents

Age is a very useful factor which indicates change in the interest of the women entrepreneurs and also influences them to start their business activities. Table 8.2 and Fig. 8.2 shows the age wise classification of the respondents.

Table 8.1. Age-wise classification

Age	Number of respondents	Percentage
Up to 20	21	17.5
20-40	62	51.7
40-60	31	25.8
Above 60	6	5
Total	**120**	**100**

Source: Primary data.

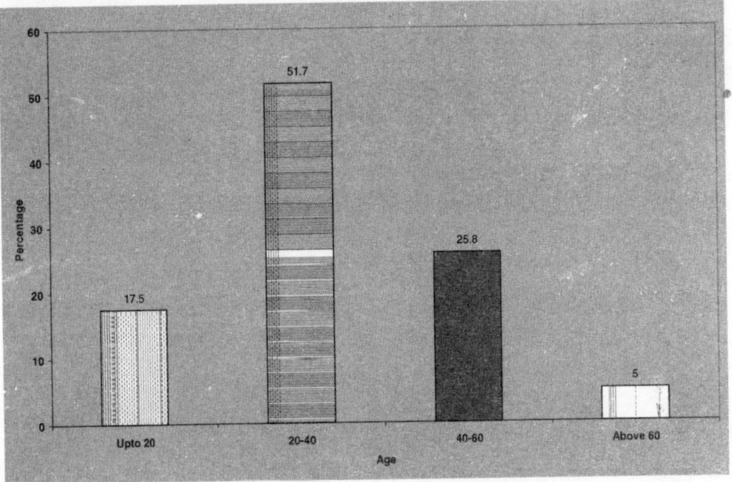

Fig. 8.1. Age-wise Classfiication

Table 8.1 Fig. 8.2 depict that out of 120 respondents 62 (51.7%) belong to the age group of 30-40 years. In the age group of 40-60 years, there are 31 (25.8%) respondents. The other, 21 (17.5%) respondents belong to the age group of upto 20 years and the remaining 6 (5%) respondents belong to the age group of above 60 years.

Educational Qualifications

Education is the primary source of knowledge and intelligence which make the person qualified and enriches the quality of the job. Table 8.2 and Fig. 8.2 reveals the educational qualification of the respondents.

Table 8.2. Educational Status of the Respondents

Educational Qualifications	Number of respondents	Percentage
No formal education	6	5
School level	75	62.5
College level	32	26.7
ITI/Diploma	7	5.8
Total	**120**	**100**

Source: Primary data.

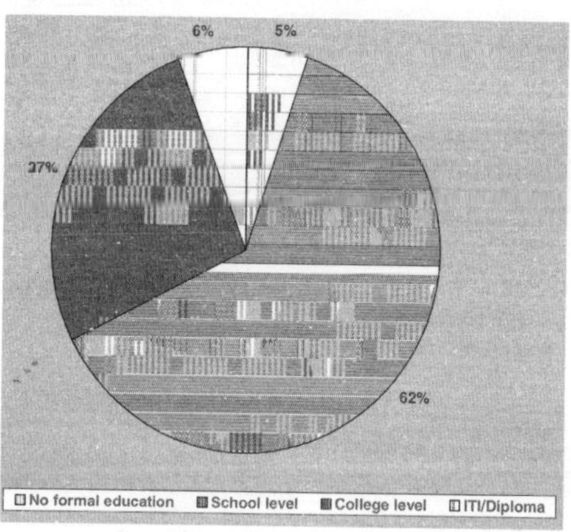

Fig. 8.2. Educational Status of the Respondents

From Table 8.2 and Fig. 8.2 it is observed that, majority of the respondents 75 (62.5%) have completed their school education. Nearly 32 respondents are graduates. Only seven (5.8%) out of 120 respondents have completed Diploma courses. The least score of 6 (5%) represents who are illiterate.

Marital Status

Marital status influences the attitude and decision taken by women entrepreneurs. Marriage brings about a turning point for some women as they tend to become entrepreneurs. Marital status of the respondents is given in Table 8.3 and Fig. 3.3.

Table 8.3. Marital Status of the Respondents

Marital Status	Number of respondents	Percentage
Married	105	87.5
Unmarried	4	3.3
Divorced	3	2.5
Widowed	8	6.7
Total	**120**	**100**

Source: Primary data.

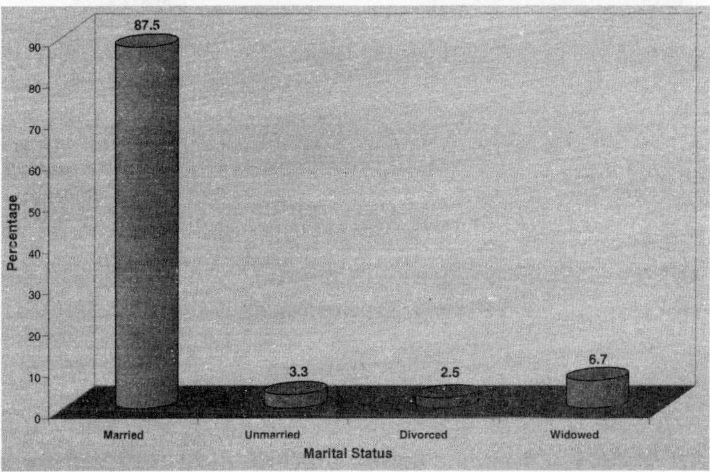

Fig. 8.3. Marital Status of the Respondents

Table 8.3 and Fig. 8.3 reveals that among 120 respondents 105 (87.5%) are married and eight (6.7%) of the respondents are widowed. Only four (3.3%) are unmarried and the respondents who are divorced are the least (2.5%).

Type of Family

Family plays an important role in determining the personality of individuals. A nuclear family is in a nurturing environment

Table 8.4. Type of Family

Type of Family	Number of respondents	Percentage
Nuclear	94	78.3
Joint	26	21.7
Total	120	100

Source: Primary data.

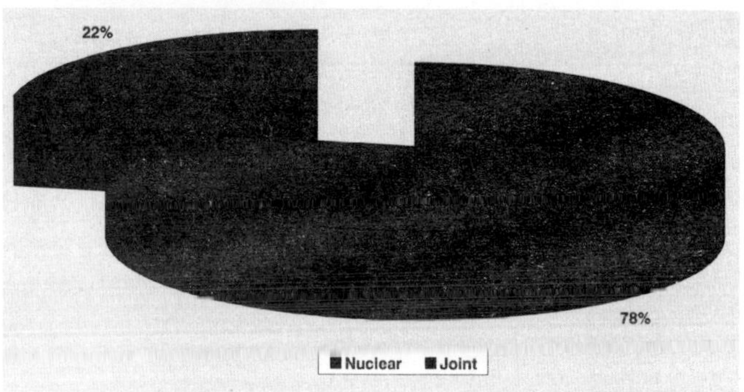

Fig. 8.4. Type of Family

in which emotional support, low stress and a stable economic environment is possible. In a nuclear family a woman has more time for herself which encourages her to enter into entrepreneurship. A joint family concerns itself arte much more matter and involvement than people living passively under the same roof. A wamen in a joint family has to spend a great deal of time for household work Table 8.4 and Fig. 8.4 shows the type of family of the respondents. Women of the modern family need only the consent of the husband to undertake responsibilities to her liking. In the joint family system, the women have to dance to the terms of the men, especially the elders. From Table 8.4 it is observed that 78.3 per cent of the respondents belong to nuclear family and only 21.7 per cent are of joint family.

Experience of the Respondents

A woman entrepreneur with work experience dishes out superior performances. Experience gives her self-confidence and risk taking abilities. The total experience of the respondents is shown in Table 8.5 and Fig. 8.5.

Table 8.5. Experience of the Respondents

Experience in years	Number of respondents	Percentage
Up to 3	18	15
3-6	45	37.5
6-9	33	27.5
Above 9	24	20
Total	**120**	**100**

Source: Primary data.

It is observed from Table 8.5 and Fig. 8.5 that 37.5 percent of the respondents are occupied with their business for a period of 3 to 6 years. The respondents carrying business between 6 to 9 years constitute 27.5 percentage. Nearly 20 per cent of the respondents are running the business for more than nine years and only 15 per cent of the respondents have experience of less than three years. This includes a fresh batch of entrepreneurs.

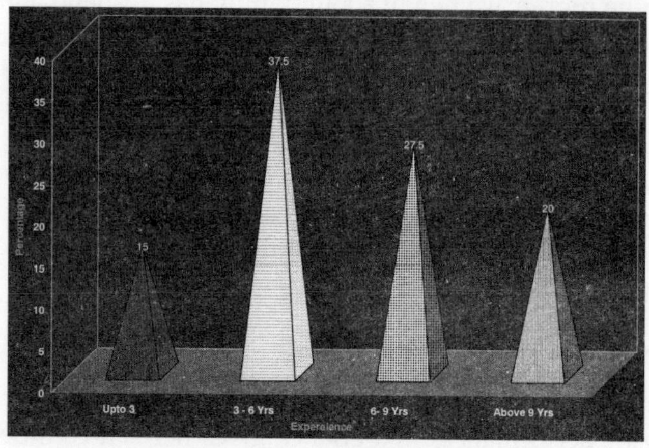

Fig. 8.5. Experience of the Respondents

Nature of Business

The nature of business has an important bearing on the choice of the form of ownership. A women entrepreneur may select a product is accordance with her capacity and motivation. Table 8.6 and Fig. 3.6 shows the nature of business of the respondents.

Table 8.6. Nature of Business

Nature of business	Number of respondents	Percentage
Consumer Goods	25	20.8
Textiles	37	30.8
Industrial products	14	11.7
Food products	30	25
Agricultural products	6	5
Cosmetics	8	6.7
Total	**120**	**100**

Source: Primary data.

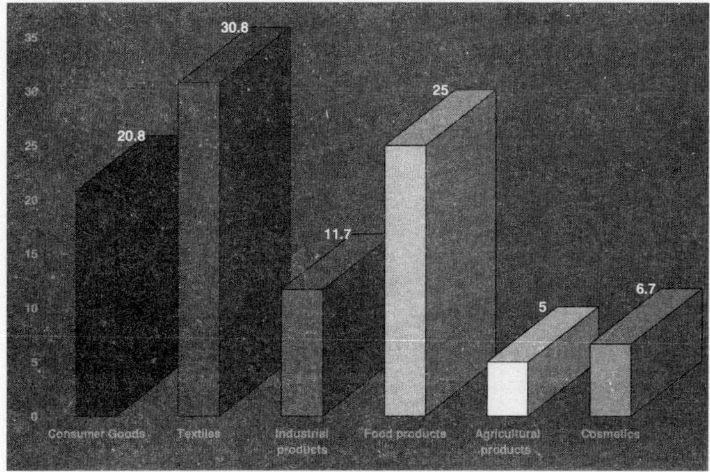

Fig. 8.6. Mature of Business

It is inferred from Table 8.6 and Fig. 8.6 that 30.8 per cent of the respondents are doing textile business. Respondents belonging to the trade of food products are 25 per cent. About 20.8 per cent of the respondents do the business of consumer goods. Nearly 6.7 per cent of the respondents are dealing with cosmetic items and 5 per cent of the respondents are dealing with agricultural products.

Source of Information

Sources are the golden main of information of a wide range. Sources are the dependable domains that provide one with information about business. Women entrepreneurs can get the necessary information through friends and relatives, newspaper, television and banks. The sources of information about business are shown in Table 8.7.

As per Table 8.7 the foremost source that provides the information about the business enterprise is friends and relatives having the weighted average score of 3.65. The second source which provides information about the business is newspaper having the weighted average score of 3.17. The third source which provides the information about business is banks having the weighted average score of 2.98. The fourth source which provides information about the business is banks having the weighted average score of 2.875. The last preference is given to DIC.

Table 8.7. Source of information

Sources of Information	Number of respondents					Weighted score	Weighted Avg.	Rank
	1	2	3	4	5			
Friends & Relatives	50	22	20	12	16	438	3.65	I
Banks	16	38	15	20	21	358	2.98	III
DIC	14	11	28	14	53	279	2.325	V
Newspaper	20	28	28	40	4	380	3.17	II
Television	20	21	29	24	26	345	2.875	IV

Source: Primary data.

Registration

To create a congenial environment for developing women entrepreneurship in rural and urban areas many institutions are set up. The main purpose of Chamber of commerce is to promote interest in local business possibilities. The District Industries Centre develops new entrepreneurs by conducting entrepreneurial motivation progorammes throughout the district. The non-governmental organization plays an important role in the lives of women in many parts of the world. The primary objective of Khadi and VillageIndustries is augmenting the employment opportunities for women. This institution inspires registered women entrepreneurs to take active participation in business. Table 8.8 and Fig. 8.7 depicts the membership details of the women entrepreneurs.

It is inferred from Table 8.8 and Fig. 8.7 that, 25 per cent of the respondents are selected from each of the institutions like Chambers of commerce, District industrial centre, Non-governmental organization, Khadi and Village Industrial Commission.

Table 8.8. Registration

Membership	Number of respondents	Percentage
Chambers of Commerce	30	25
District Industries Centre	30	25
Non-governmental Organisation	30	25
Khadi and Village Industrial Commission	30	25
Total	**120**	**100**

Source: Primary data.

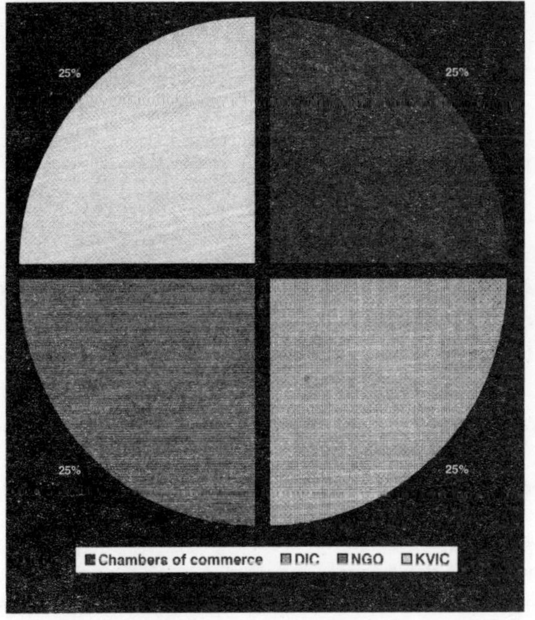

Fig. 8.7. Registration

Form of Ownership

Business units are different types such as a sole trader concern, partnership firm, and private limited company. A sole proprietorship is a type of business entity which is owned and run by one individual and where there is no legal distinction between the owner and the business. A partnership is a type of business entity in which the owners/partners share with each other the profits or loss of the business. A company is a form of business organization. The following Table 8.9 presents the classification of enterprise on the basis of type of organization.

Table 8.9. Form of Ownership

Form of ownership	Number of respondents	Percentage
Sole proprietorship	97	80.8
Partnership	20	16.7
Private limited company	3	2.5
Total	120	100

Source: Primary data.

It is seen from Table 8.9 that, 97 per cent of the sample units are functioning on sole proprietorship basis and 20 per cent are of partnership firms. An enterprise functioning as private limited company is accounted for 2.5 per cent. This has been due to the fact that starting of sole trader organizations is easy unlike the joint stock companies where lot of legal formalities are to be observed.

Investment Pattern

The amount of investment is likely to influence the efficiency of the firm and their performance. On the one hand, low level of investment may not give any scope for innovation, market expansion etc. while on the other, the operational constraints amount up for those investing higher amount. The level of investment is given in Table 8.10.

It seen from Table 8.10 that, 35 per cent of the women entrepreneurs are having the investment of above Rs. 60,000.

Nearly one-fourth respondents are having the investment upto Rs. 20,000. Respondents having investment between Rs. 40,000 to Rs. 60,000 is 23.3 per cent and 16.7 per cent of the respondents are having the investment between Rs. 20,000 to Rs. 40,000.

Table 8.10. Investment Pattern

Investment	Number of respondents	Percentage
Up to Rs. 20,000	30	25
Rs. 20,000-Rs. 40,000	20	16.7
Rs. 40,000-Rs. 60,000	28	23.3
Above Rs. 60,000	42	35
Total	**120**	**100**

Source: Primary data.

Borrowings

Women entrepreneurs in middle income or low income group depend on borrowed fund to start their enterprise or expansion of the business units. They used to borrow fund for their business units. Table 8.11 shows the borrowings of the respondents.

Table 8.11. Borrowings

Borrowings	Number of respondents	Percentage
Yes	73	60.83
No	47	39.2
Total	**120**	**100**

Source: Primary data.

It is observed from Table 8.11 that, out of 120 respondents 73 (60.83%) have availed of loan for their business and the remaining 39.2 per cent of the respondents have not borrowed any funds.

Source of Borrowings

Business units used to borrow fund from friends and relatives or from bank and financial institutions. The money lender offers small personal loan at high interest rate. A financial institution is an institution that provides financial services for its clients or members. Table 8.12 shows the source of borrowing.

Table 8.12. Source of borrowings

Source Borrowings	Number of respondents					Intensity value	Rank
	1	2	3	4	5		
Relatives	9	21	12	16	15	212	III
Friends	3	12	27	16	15	191	IV
Banks	40	16	8	7	2	291	I
Financial institution	6	10	10	16	31	163	V
Money lender	13	14	16	18	12	217	II

Source: Primary data.

On the basis of the rank given by the respondents the bank plays an important role for providing funds for the business. It has a high intensity value of 291.The second important source of borrowing is from the money lender with the intensity value of 217. The third source of borrowing is from the relatives with the intensity value of 212. The fourth source of borrowing is from the friends with the intensity value of 191. The last source of borrowing is from the financial institutions with intensity value 163.

Type of Family and Nature of Business

To analyse the relationship between the type of family and the nature of business the Chi-square test is applied by framing the hypothsis such as,

H_0 – There is no relationship between the type of family and nature of business of the respondents

H_a – There is a relationship between the type of family and nature of business of the respondents

Table 8.13. Type of family and nature of business

Type of family	Nature of business						Total
	Consumer goods	Textiles	Industrial products	Food products	Agricultural products	cosmetics	
Nuclear family	20	27	12	23	6	6	94
Joint family	5	10	2	7	-	2	26
Total	25	37	14	30	6	8	120

Source: Primary data.

The result of Chi-square test is presented in Table 8.13(a)

Table 8.13(a).

χ^2 calculated value	1.335	Degrees of freedom	5	Table value @ 5 per cent level of significance

Since the calculated value χ^2 (1.335) at five per cent level of significance (d.f=5) is less than the Table value (11.1), the null hypothesis is accepted. Thus it is inferred that, there is no relationship between the type of family and nature of business of the respondents.

Factor Anlaysis

Factor motivating women entrepreneurs to start an enterprise can vary depending on the nature of business activities. Certain statements relating to women entrepreneurs were given to the respondents and their opinions were obtained. Factor analysis technique has been used to find out the fundamental officers that create community among the statements. By using factor analysis the number of statements can be reduced in terms of a few categories, which are called factors, and these factors are selected and studied in this chapter.

The opinions of the respondents are studied with regard to the motivating factors for women to become an entrepreneur.

Factor analysis is a technique used in identifying a smaller number of factors underlying a large number of observed variables. Variables that have a high correlation between them, and are largely independent of other subsets of variables, are combined into factors.

Mathematically factor anlaysis is somewhat similar to multiple regression analysis in that each variable is expressed as a linear in that each variable is expressed as a linear combination of underlying factors. The amount of variance a variable shares with all other variables included in the analysis is referred to as communality. The co variation among the variables is described in terms of a small number of common factors plus a unique factor for each variable.

The first stage in factor analysis is the factor extraction process, where the objective is to identity how many factors will be extracted from the data and that is done by using principal components anlaysis. The extraction of factors depends upon the eigen values. The higher the eigen value of the factor, the higher is the amount of variance explained by the factors.

The second stage is the rotation of principal components that identifies which factors are associated with which of the original variables. The loading of each variable on each of the extracted factors given by the rotated factor matrix value close to represent high loadings and those close 1 to 0 represents low loadings. The main objective of the study is to find out the variables which have a high loading on one factor but low loadings on other factors.

In this study the rotated sum of squared loadings indicated that five statements are enough to explain 65 per cent of the opinion. The eigen values are given in Table 8.15.

Table 8.14. The Initial Eigen Value

Component	Initial Eigen Value		
	Total	Percentage of Variance	Cumulative
1	3.743	23.394	23.394
2	1.946	12.163	35.557
3	1.866	11.663	47.220
4	1.628	10.174	57.395
5	1.232	7.699	65.093
6	0.912	5.697	70.791
7	0.880	5.499	76.290
8	0.666	4.164	80.454
9	0.582	3.637	84.091
10	0.519	3.245	87.336
11	0.494	3.090	90.426
12	0.420	2.623	93.049
13	0.397	2.484	95.533
14	0.280	1.752	97.285
15	0.240	1.501	98.786
16	0.194	1.214	100.00

The rotated sums of squared loadings are given in Table 8.16.

Table 8.15. Rotated Sums of Squared Loadings

Factors	Total	Percentage of Variance	Cumulative Percentage
1.	2.302	14.384	14.389
2.	2.204	13.776	28.650
3.	2.190	13.690	41.854
4.	1.951	12.191	54.046
5.	1.768	11.048	65.093

The rotated factor matrix with communalities are given in Table 8.16.

Table 8.16. Rotated Factor Matrix

Variables	Factor I	Factor II	Factor III	Factor IV	Factor V	Factor VI	Commu-nalities
Desire to generate new ideas	.902						0.852
To be independent	.823						0.740
Willingness to grow	.775						0.646
Successfully managing myself		.821					0.697
Ability to withstand difficult situation		.720					0.630
Successfully managing others		.703					0.611
Decision making capacity		.614					0.475
To earn more money			.854				0.764
To satisfy the needs			.795				0.760
Creativity			.760				0.625
To be prestigious				.799			0.667
To enjoy esteem				.790			0.643
To get recognition				.548			0.594
Emotional stability						.835	0.722
Capacity to achieve goal						.739	0.619
Government incentives and concession						.463	0.367

*The value 0.80 is taken as cut off point.

From the rotated factor matrix it is noticed that seven statements have come under factor 1 with high factor loadings.

Table 8.17 depicts the statements with factor loadings.

Table 8.17. Factor I - Statements with High Loadings

Statement	Factor Loadings
Desire to generate new ideas	0.902
To be independent	0.823
Willingness to grow	0.755

All the related variables are combined into a common factor called 'Innovative motive'. The variables indicating the autonomy are "desire to generate new ideas", "to be independent" and "willingness to grow". The innovative motive is the prime motivator of entrepreneurial behaviour.

It is also clear from the three selected factors, the first statement 'the desire to generate new ideas' is the prime motivator for the women entrepreneurs that have high factor loading close to 1. It is interpreted that 90 per cent of the respondents feel that 'desire to generate new ideas' is the factor motivating women to become entrepreneurs.

From the related factor matrix it is seen that five statements have come under factor two with high factor loading. Table 8.18 shows the statements with factor loadings.

Table 8.18. Factor – II Statements With High Loadings

Statement	Factor Loadings
Successfully managing myself	.821
Ability to withstand difficult situation	.720
Successfully managing others	.703
Decision making capacity	.614

All these related variables are combined into a common factor called 'power motive'. The power motive includes the factors like 'successfully managing myself', 'ability to withstand difficult situation', 'successfully managing others' and 'decision making capacity'.

It is also clear from the four statements; the first statements such as "successfully managing myself" has high factor loadings close to 1. It is interpreted that 82 percent of the respondents have capacity to manage themselves successfully.

From the rotated factor matrix it depicts that three statements have come under factor III with high factor loadings. Table 8.19 shows the statements with factor loadings.

Table 8.19. Factor III: Statements with High Loadings

Statement	Factor Loadings
To earn more money	.854
To satisfy the needs	.795
Creativity	.760

All these related variables are combined into common factor called 'self-actualization motive'. Self-actualization is an individual's motive to transform her perception of self into reality and it is the acme of human motivation to become or achieve what one can.

It is also clear from the statements that earning more money also motivates the women to become an entrepreneur. It is interpreted that 85 per cent of the respondents have shown their preference for making more money.

From the rotated factor matrix it is discerned that two statements have come under factor III with high factor loadings. Table 8.20 shows the statements with high factor loadings.

Table 8.20. Factor – IV: Statements with High Loadings

Statement	Factor Loadings
To be prestigious	.799
To enjoy esteem	.790
To get recognition	.548

All these related variables are combined into a common factor called 'status motive'. Social status implies the standing or the place of people in their society. It refers to social status and the resultant self-esteem and influence.

It also describes from the first two statements such as 'to be prestigious and enjoy esteem' have high factor loading close to 1. These two statements have more or less the same factor loadings. It is interpreted that 79 per cent of the respondents have shown their preference for prestige and esteem.

From the rotated factor matrix it is seen that, two statements have come under factor V with high factor loadings. Table 8.21 exhibits the statements with high factor loadings.

Table 8.21. Factor V: Statements with high loadings

Statement	Factor Loadings
Emotional stability	.835
Capacity to achieve goal	.739

All these related variables are combined into a common factor called 'success motive'. Success motive includes 'emotional stability' and 'capacity to achieve goal'.

It is also clear that those two statements such as 'emotional stability' and 'capacity to achieve goal' have high factor loadings close to 1.It is interpreted that 83 percent of the respondents have emotional stability in their business.

Conclusion

The major motivational factors for entrepreneurs to start their own enterprise were autonomy motive, power motive, self-actualization motive, status motive and success motive.

REFERENCES

1. Women entrepreneurs in the informal sector: A Study of Kerala, *Southern Economists* Vol. 38, No.15 and 16, Dec 1999, pp. 23-24.
2. *Perspectives of women entrepreneurship*, Sobha Rani, B, Koteswara Rao.D. Social Welfare. July-Aug. 2008.
3. Women entrepreneurship in India, *Southern Economists*, Vol. 38, No.1-4 , June 15,1999, pp. 11.

CHAPTER

Problems of Women Enterpreneurs

Introduction

Women owned businesses are exhibiting an incredibly expansive trend in the economies of almost all countries. The hidden entrepreneurial potentials of women have gradually been changing with the growing sensitivity to the role and economic status in the society. Skills, knowledge and adaptability in business are the main reasons for women to emerge into business ventures. Woman entrepreneur is a person who accepts challenging role to meet her personal needs and become economically independent. A strong desire to do something positive is an inbuilt quality of entrepreneurial women, who are capable of contributing values in both family and social life. With the advent of media, women are aware of their own traits, rights and also the work situations. The glass ceilings are shattered and women are found pursuing in every line of business from pappad to power cables.

This chapter has made an attempt to analyse the,

- Training and earnings of the respondents
- Problems in starting the business
- Problems in running the business

- Marketing problems
- Problems in getting the finance
- Marketability of products
- Advertising media
- Export of the product and countries of exports

Training

Training helps a person in strengthening their entrepreneurial motive and in acquiring skills and capabilities necessary for playing their entrepreneurial role effectively. Training is essential for the development of entrepreneurship. Table 9.1 show the training background.

Table 9.1. Training

Training	Number of respondents	Percentage
Yes	62	51.67
No	58	48.33
Total	120	100

Source: Primary data.

It is seen from Table 9.1 and Fig. 9.1 that, only 62 (51.67%) respondents have undergone training and the remaining 58 (48.33%) respondents have not attended any training programme.

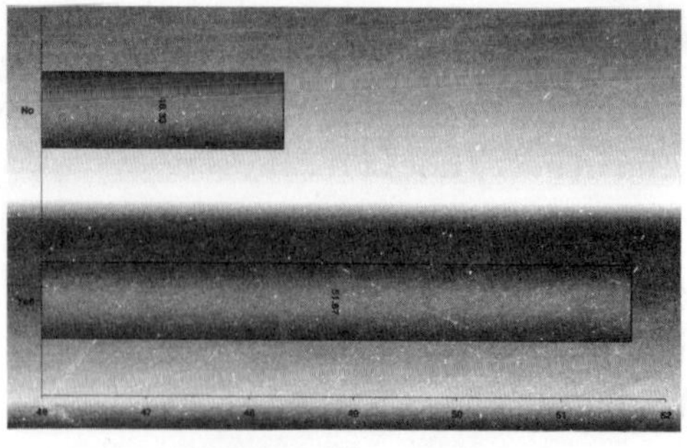

Fig. 9.1. Training

Earnings of the Respondents

Earnings bring financial stability in the business as well as in the family. It also gives prestige, power, independence and initiative among women entrepreneurs. Table 9.2 and Fig. 9.2 shows the earnings of the respondents.

Table 9.2. Earnings of the Respondents

Earning	Number of respondents	Percentage
Up to Rs. 5,000	49	41
Rs. 5,000-Rs. 10,000	28	23
Rs.10,000-Rs. 15,000	18	15
Above Rs. 15,000	25	21
Total	120	100

Source: Primary data.

From Table 9.2 and Fig. 9.2 it is revealed that, 49 (41%) of the respondents are earning upto Rs. 5,000. About 23 per cent and 21 per cent of the respondents have earned between Rs. 5,000 and Rs. 10,000 and above Rs. 15,000 respectively. However, 15 per cent of the respondents are have earnings between Rs. 10,000 and Rs. 15,000.

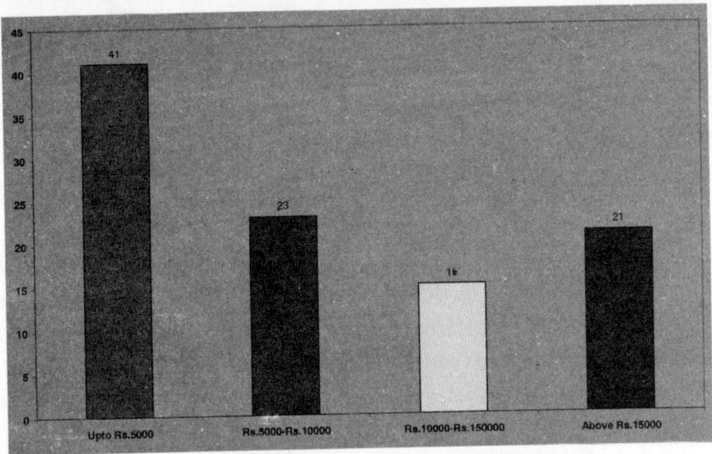

Fig. 9.2. Earnings of the respondents

Problems in Starting the Business

For many women the first plunge into business is a real challenge. Rapid economic, technological and social change has an impact on the nature of the organization and their work. Finance is a must for kickstarting a new venture. Adequate finance is essential for entrepreneurs to protect their business from financial crises. Lack of finance forces the women entrepreneurs to compromise with their dreams.[1] The main challenge a women faces in her career comes from the family.

Table 9.3. Problems in starting the business

Factors	Rank						Garret's score	Average score	Rank
	1	2	3	4	5	6			
Lack of finance	30	32	25	13	4	16	6790	56.58	II
Lack of support from family	13	10	19	24	30	24	5423	45.19	V
Lack of labour	32	33	16	17	13	9	6877	57.31	I
Lack of entrepreneurial awareness	21	20	24	17	17	21	5982	49.85	III
Lack of infrastructure	17	19	16	23	24	21	5799	48.33	IV
Combining family and work life	7	6	20	26	32	29	5044	42.03	VI

Source: Primary data.

The family members are not generally supportive enough and also the family responsibilities restrict them from giving their best to the work field.[2] The increasing emphasis on providing more value added products creates the demand for skilled labour. Women in business face an acute shortage of labour.[3] The entrepreneurs sometimes are aware of the social environment where they are, and also of the culture of the society which discourages women. They lack awareness in contributing to managerial skill, leadership and entrepreneurial goal.[4] Inadequate infrastructure is one of the principal risk factors the companies face while doing the business. The major hurdle for women in business is to combine the family and the enterprise. Table 9.3 shows the problems in starting the business.

Analysis of factors in Table 9.3 shows that, lack of labour is the first problem (Garret's score of 6877) followed by lack of finance (Garret's score of 6790). Lack of entrepreneurial awareness occupies the third place with the Garret's score of 5982. Lack of infrastructure is in the fourth place with the Garret's score of 5799 and lack of support from family takes fifth place with the Garret's score of 5423. Combining family and work life stands last with the Garret's score of 5044.

Problems in Running the Business

Women get no assistance and encouragement to start and run the business. Inspite of that, compared to men women alone in most of the cases shoulder both business and family responsibilities. The business run by women gets struck many times because of inadequate availability of finance. As women in business, they play a dual role with business and family, and time becomes scarce for them (Table 9.4). Business problems are distinct from family problems and so women entrepreneurs while running the business, face the difficulty of managing both. Being women the distance matters a lot as far as business is concerned. The major aspects of receiving the business order is, 'getting to know each other' which becomes rare for many of the women entrepreneurs.[5]

H_0 – There is no significant relationship in ranks assigned by different respondents regarding the problems in running the business.

H_a – There is a significant relationship in ranks assigned by different respondents regarding the problems in running the business.

Table 9.4. Problem in running the business

Factors	Rank						Total
	1	2	3	4	5	6	
Gender discrimination	30	32	25	13	4	16	120
Financial problems	13	10	19	24	30	24	120
Less availability of time	32	33	16	17	13	9	120
Difficulties in managing business and family	21	20	24	17	17	21	120
Less accessability	17	19	16	23	24	21	120
Difficulties in getting the order	7	6	20	26	32	29	120
Total	120	120	120	120	120	120	

Source: Primary data.

As there are six sets of ranking, the coefficient of concordance (W) for judging significant agreement in ranking by different respondents is worked out by using the formula,

$$W = \frac{S}{1/12k^2\left(N^3 - N\right)}$$

The calculated value of S = 41,348

W= 0.164

To judge the significance of W the table value at five per cent level of significance is 221.4 and the calculated value is 41,348. The calculated value is more than the table value. Hence the null hypothesis is rejected and it is infered that there is a significant relationship in ranks assigned by different respondents regarding the problem in running the business.

Marketing Problem

A business is an organized effort to sell products and services on a regular basis. Women entrepreneurs face difficulty in marketing their products due to lack of knowledge. Competition between business and sores consists of trying to get the customers to buy their products. In marketing their products some women depend on local market and sometimes a middleman misuses the market. The marketing problems are shown in Table 9.5

Table 9.5. Problems in Marketing

Problem in marketing	Number of respondents					Intensity Value	Rank
Lack of knowledge about the market	10	27	12	36	25	301	VII
Relying on local market.	17	82	10	4	7	458	IV
Competition	43	54	14	6	3	488	II
Exploitation by middlemen	18	40	53	4	5	422	VI
Difficulty in collectingthe dues	50	40	11	13	6	475	III
Inadequate sales promotion avenues	26	60	23	7	4	757	I
Lack of export market support	25	46	41	2	6	442	V

Source: Primary data.

On the basis of the ranks given by the respondents inadequate sales promotion avenues is the foremost reason cited by the respondents for marketing the product, with the highest intensity value of 757. Heavy competition from big enterprises stands second with the intensity value of 488. Difficulties in the collection of dues are the third reason mentioned with the intensity value of 475 and relaying on local market is also one of the marketing problems with the intensity value of 458. Lack of export market support (intensity value 442) and exploitation by middlemen (intensity value 422) are also the problems in marketing. Lack of enough knowledge about the market has got the lowest intensity value of 301.

Problem in Getting Finance

Finance is the lifeblood of business and it severs as the lubricant for the wheel of business machinery. Financial problem is a major problem faced by all respondents. Financial

Table 9.6. Problems in getting finance

Factor	Number of Respondents							Garret's score	Average score	Rank
	1	2	3	4	5	6	7			
Very long procedure	13	20	25	31	17	4	10	6386	53.22	III
Unnecessary documents	20	27	34	16	11	9	3	6922	57.68	I
Insufficient assistance	13	22	18	23	22	14	8	6232	51.93	V
Officers arenot helpful	13	26	20	16	21	16	8	6285	52.38	IV
High interestrate	40	16	14	13	17	7	13	6866	57.22	II
Difficult to go forrefinance	4	6	2	6	16	47	39	4227	35.23	VII
Waste of timeenergy & money	17	3	7	15	16	23	39	4962	41.35	VI

Source: Primary data.

problems are faced at the time of starting the business as well as during operation of their business enterprise. Insufficient financial support is the most important problem. Financial support given by the government agencies is inadequate. Women entrepreneurs are not able to get financial assistance from banks as there are complex procedures and security problems. Table 9.6 shows the problems in getting the finance.

Analysis of factors in Table 9.6 brings to light the rank order for the financial problems. 'Unnecessary documents' are ranked first with Garret's score at 6922 which is followed by high interest rate (Garret's score at 6866). 'Very long procedure' gets the third place with the Garret's score of 6386. Unhelpful officers and insufficient assistance provided get the fourth and the fifth place with the Garret's score of 6285 and 6232 respectively. 'Waste of time, energy and money' is ranked sixth with Garret's score of 4962 and 'difficult to go for refinance' has got the last place with the Garret's score of 4227.

Time Spent

Time spent is a very important factor which determines the success of the enterprise. Table 9.7 give and Fig. 9.3 the details regarding the working hours of the respondents.

Table 9.7. Time spent for business

Time Spent (Hrs)	Number of respondents	Percentage
Upto 4	28	23
4-8	30	25
8-12	37	31
Above 12	25	21
Total	**120**	**100**

Source: Primary data.

Table 9.7 and Fig. 9.3 depict that 31 per cent of the respondents are likely to spend 8 to 12 hours per day. 25 percent of the respondents are working for only 4 to 8 hours and 23 per cent of the respondents spend only below 4 hours. Only 21 per cent of the respondents work above 12 hours per day.

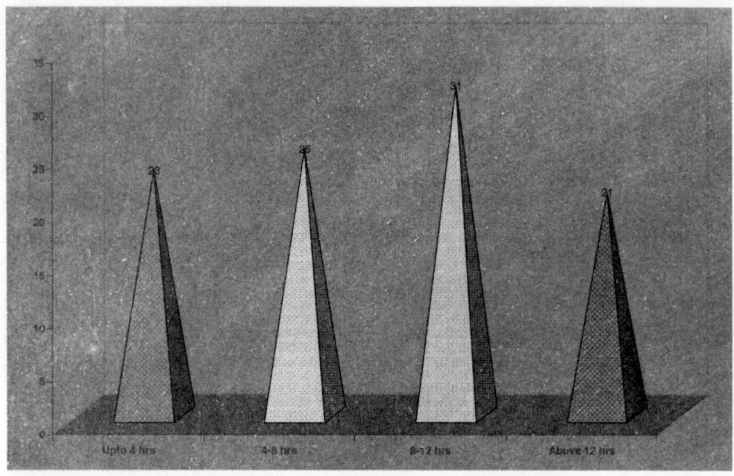

Fig. 9.3. Time spent for business

Type of Family and Time Spent

Table 9.8. Type of family and time spent

Type of family	Time spent				Total
	Upto 4 hrs	4-8 hrs	8-12 hrs	Above 12 hrs	
Nuclear family	23	22	32	17	94
Joint family	5	8	5	8	26
Total	**28**	**30**	**37**	**25**	**120**

Source: Primary data.

To analyse the relationship between the type of family and the time spent the Chi-square test is applied by framing the hypothesis such as,

H_0 – There is no relationship between the type of family and working hours of the respondents.

H_a – There is a relationship between the type of family and working hours of the respondents.

The result of Chi-square test is presented in Table 9.8(a).

Table 9.8(a)

χ^2 calculated value	3.715	Degrees of freedom	3	Table value @ 5 per cent level of significance

Since the calculated value χ^2 (3.715) at 5 percent level of significance (d.f=3) is less than the table value (7.81), the null hypothesis is accepted. Thus it is inferred that, there is no relationship between the type of family and working hours of the respondents.

Nature of Business and Time Spent

On the basis of the nature of business the working hour differs.

Table 9.9 shows the relationship between working hours and nature of business of the respondents.

Table 9.9. Nature of business and time spent

Nature of business	Time Spent				Total
	Up to 4 hrs	4-8 h	8-12 h	Above 12 h	
Consumer goods	5	6	7	7	25
Textiles	12	10	9	6	37
Industrial products	2	5	5	2	14
Food products	3	4	14	9	30
Agricultural products	2	3	1	-	6
Cosmetics	4	2	1	1	8
Total	**28**	**30**	**37**	**25**	**120**

H_0 – There is no relationship between the nature of business and time spent by the respondents.

H_a – There is a relationship between the nature of business and time spent by the respondents.

To test the difference in the single dependent variable time spent among the six groups formed by single independent variable, One-Way ANOVA is used [Table 9.9(a)].

Table 9.9(a). One Way ANOVA

Source of Variation	Sum of Square	V	Mean Sqaure	F
Between groups	197.5	5	39.5	$F = \frac{39.5}{6.58}$
Within group	118.5	18	6.58	=6.003
Total	**316**	**23**		

As the calculated value (6.003) is more than the table value of F for $V_1 = 5$ and $V_2=18$ at 5% level of significance (4.25), the null hypothesis is rejected. Thus it is inferred that, there is a significant difference between working hours and nature of business of the respondents.

Marketability of Products

Marketing is the managerial process through which products are matched with markets. The success of business firms greatly depends upon how best they serve and satisfy their customers. Selection of place or area where the women entrepreneurs are going to sell their products is an important

Table 9.10. Marketability of Products

Marketability of Products	Number of respondents	Percentage
Madurai District	87	72.5
Other Districts	18	15
National	5	4.17
International	10	8.33
Total	**120**	**100**

Source: Primary data.

factor regarding the marketability of products. Table 9.10 show the extent of marketability of products.

It is inferred from Table 9.10 and Fig. 9.4 that, 72.5 percent of the respondents market their products in Madurai district only. The respondents who have reached markets in other districts are 18. Nearly 10 respondents are doing their business at international level. Only 4.17 percent of the respondents market their products at national level.

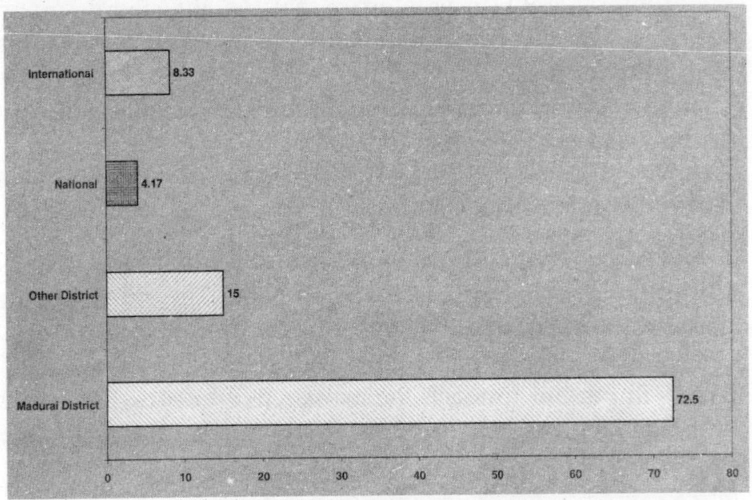

Fig. 9.4. Marketability of Products

Multiple Regression Analysis

Multiple Regression analysis is used to analyse the relationship between extent of marketability, the dependent variable which is based on the independent variables such as educational qualification and experience.

H_0 -The extent of marketability of product is not positively related to its educational qualification and is also related to its experience.

H_a –The extent of marketability of product is positively related to its educational qualification and also related to its experience.

The formula for multiple regression equation is

$$v = a + b_1x_1 + b_2x_2$$

The result is presented in table 9.11

Table 9.11

R	R Square	Adjusted R Square	Std. Error of the estimate
0.995	0.990	0.969	6.77402

From Table 9.11 it is inferred that the adjusted R square value is 0.969. It us seen that the independent variables educational qualification and experience account for 96.9% relationship on the dependent variable, that is marketability of the products.

Advertising Media

Advertising media is a means through which advertisers communicate their ideas to customers. The media gives detailed information about the enterprises and the products. Selection of appropriate media for different kinds of products is also important to reach the prospective buyers. Table 9.12 and Fig. 9.5 gives details regarding the media of advertising.

Table 9.12. Advertising Media

Media	Number of respondents	Percentago
Television	2	1.6
Newspaper	16	13.33
Radio	3	2.5
None	99	82.5
Total	**120**	**100**

Source: Primary data.

It is noticed from Table 9.12 and Fig. 9.5 that, out of 120 respondents 99 (82.5%) have not selected any media to advertise their products. Only 16 (13.33%) respondents have advertised their business in the newspapers. Radio advertisement is followed only by three respondents. Only two respondents have advertised through television as it is a costly media.

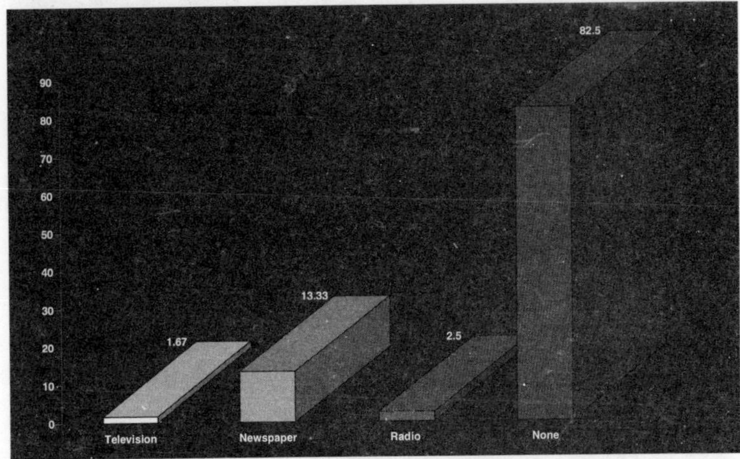

Fig. 9.5. Advertising Media

Export

The term export is derived from the conceptual meaning as to ship the goods and services out of the port of a country. A potential exporter needs to keep a keen and open mind to look for opportunities and generate business ideas in utilizing skills and services, available resources, raw materials and technology or other possibilities. Table 9.13 and Fig. 9.6 shows the nature of the export.

Table 9.13. Export

Export	Number of respondents	Percentage
Yes	10	8.33
No	110	91.67
Total	**120**	**100**

Source: Primary data.

It is noticed that out of 120 respondents 10(8.33) are exporting their product to outside countries. The large majority of the respondents do business inside the country only.

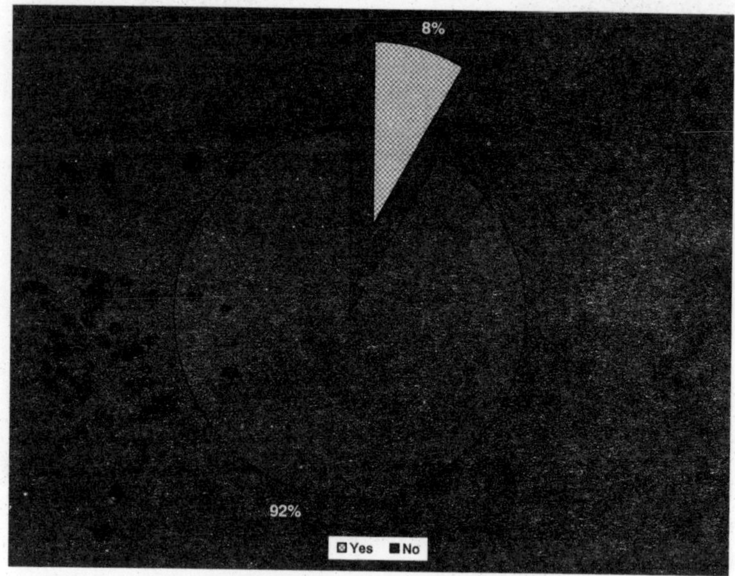

Fig. 9.6. Export of the products

Exports by Women Entrepreneurs

'Women in Export' programme aims to help women business leaders realise their full export potential by encouraging

Table 9.14. Export by women entrepreneurs

Export product	Number of respondents	Percentage
Consumer goods	1	10
Textiles	7	70
Food products	2	20
Total	**10**	**100**

Source: Primary data.

businesswomen and businesses owned or operated by women to export. Identifying business women who are active in export and who could become role models for other women in business and in working with existing women's networks help them achieve a greater export.[6] Table 9.14 shows the nature of export by women entrepreneurs.

From Table 9.14 it is interesting to note that out of the selected women entrepreneurs, ten are exporting their products abroad. Out of 10 export women entrepreneurs, seven (70%) export textile products and nearly two (20%) export food products. Only one (10%) exports consumer goods abroad.

Countries of Export

From Table 9.15 it is seen that, out of 10 women entrepreneurs exporting goods to foreign countries, 7 (70%) of them export their products to two destinations abroad. The number of women entrepreneurs exporting to more than two countries is only 3 (30%) which denotes that the women entrepreneurs are yet to reach other export destinations.

Table 9.15. Countries of Export

Number of countries	Number of respondents	Percentage
Upto 2	7	70
Above 2	3	30
Total	**10**	**100**

Source: Primary data.

Export Problems

Women are also the most significant contributor in the field of India's exports. There has been prominent increase in the export form the sector of both traditional and non-traditional goods including Jewellary, Garments, Leathers, hand tool's, handicrafts etc. Also, the enterprises with good performance have greatest stability in the economy. But there are a still lot of problems in exporting the products by the women entrepreneurs to other region/country/areas. There are not familiar with the steps and formalities involved in exporting goods form India. They need to aware of all the steps involved in the process of exporting the products.

Table 9.16. Export Problems

Problems	Mean	S.D
Lack of required export knowledge	4.2	1.229273
Lack of finance	3.7	1.337494
Non-availability of staff with export knowledge	3.5	1.354006
Cumbersome export documentation	3.4	1.712698
High transportation cost	3.3	1.159502
Difficult to accomplish foreign buyers expectations	3.2	1.47573
Risk involved in selling abroad	3.1	1.66333
Exchange rate fluctuations	3	1.763834
Less production capacity	2.8	1.619328
Competition from firms in foreign markets	2.6	1.074968

Source: Primary data.

On the basis of the rank given by respondents lack of required export knowledge gets a mean score of 4.2 with the standard deviation of 1.229. Lack of finance obtains a mean score of 3.7 with the standard deviation of 1.337. Non-availability of staff with export knowledge acquires a mean score of 3.5 with the standard deviation of 1.354. Cumbersome export documentation gets a mean score of 3.4 with the standard deviation of 1.713. High transportation cost obtains a mean score of 3.2 with standard deviation of 1.159. The least score gain by less production capacity followed by competition from firms in foreign markets with the standard deviation of 1.619 and 1.075.

Conclution

Women in India no longer remain confined to within four walls of house. They are participating and performing well in all spheres of activities such as academic, political, administration, space and industry.

REFERENCES

1. www.wsicorporate.com
2. www.indiaedunews.com
3. www.thehindubusinessline.com
4. www.thaindia.com
5. Women entrepreneurial Development –Dr.Sujatha.V, Gomathi.V, Savithri.N, Parveen Banu.M.A.
6. www.importexporthelp.com.

CHAPTER

Summary of Findings, Suggestions and Conclusions

Introduction

Women constitute around half of the total world population. They are regarded as the better half of the society. In traditional societies, they were confined to the four walls of houses performing household activities. In modern societies, they have come out of the four walls to participate in all sorts of activities. The global evidences buttress that women have been performing exceedingly well in different spheres of activities like academics, polities, administration, social work and so on. Now, they have started plunging into industry also and have been running their enterprises successfully.

In the present study an attempt is made to provide an analysis of women entrepreneurs with regard to the following aspects.

- Factors motivating women to become an entrepreneur.
- Problems faced by the women entrepreneurs.

Findings

- Majority of the respondents (51.7%) fall in the age group of 20-40 years.

- Majority of the respondents 75 (62.5%) have completed their school level.
- Most of the respondents 105 (87.5%) are married.
- Majority of the respondents (78.3%) are belonging to nuclear families.
- Most of the respondents (37.5%) are occupied with their business for a period of 3 to 6 years.
- Most of the respondents (30.8%) are doing textile business.
- The foremost source that provides the information about the business enterprise is friends and relatives with the weighted average score of 3.65.
- All the members are registered business enterprises. About 25 percent of the respondents are selected from each of the institution like Chambers of commerce, District Industrial Centre, Non-governmental organization, khadi and village industrial commission.
- Most of the respondents (80.8%) are functioning as sole proprietorship organizations.
- Majority of the respondents (35%) are having the investment of above Rs. 60,000.
- Most of the respondents (60.83%) have availed of loan for their business.
- While analyzing the sources of borrowing majority of the respondents felt that bank is the first source of borrowing with the intensity value of 291.
- To analyse the relationship between the type of family and the nature of business the Chi-square test is applied. The hypothesis is proved that there is no relationship between the type of family and nature of business of the respondents.
- The application of factor analysis technique showed that autonomy motive, power motive, self-actualization motive, status motive and success motive

are the main factors and related factors motivating women entrepreneurs. Among the factors rotated under autonomy motive 'Desire to generate new ideas' is the highest loaded factor besides, under power motive 'Successfully managing myself', under self-actualization motive' To earn more money', under status motive 'To be prestigious' and success motive 'Emotional stability'.

- Most of the respondents 62 (51.67%) are getting trained.
- Most of the respondents 49 (41%) are earning up to 5000 only.
- Regarding the problem faced by the women entrepreneurs while starting the business the high score of Garret's rank (6877) is given to lack of labours.
- To judge the significance of W the table value at five per cent level of significance is 221.4 and the calculated value is 41,348. The calculated value is more than the table value. Hence the null hypothesis is rejected and infers that there is a significant relationship in ranks assigned by different respondents regarding the problem in running the business.
- On the basis of the ranks given by the respondents inadequate sales promotion avenues is the foremost reason cited by the respondents for marketing the product, with the highest intensity value of 757.
- While performing analysis of factors in financial problems "Unnecessary documents" is ranked first with Garret's score at 6622.
- Most of the respondents (31%) are working 8 to 12 hours per day.
- To analyse the relationship between the type of family and the time spent the Chi-square test is applied. The hypothesis is proved that there is no relationship

between the type of family and working hours of the respondents.

- To test the difference in the single dependent variable time spent among the six groups formed by single independent variable, One-Way ANOVA is used. The hypothesis is proved that there is a significant difference between nature of business and time spent by the respondents.
- Majority of the respondents (72.5%) market their products in Madurai district only.
- Multiple Regression analysis is used to analyse the relationship between extent of marketability, the dependent variable which is based on the independent variables such as educational qualification and experience. The result of adjusted R square value is 0.969. It is seen that the independent variables educational qualification and experience account for 96.9% relationship on the dependent variable that is marketability of the products.
- Most of the respondents 99 (82.5%) are not select any media to advertise their product.
- Majority of the respondents (91.67%) do not exporting their product.
- It is interesting to note that out of the selected women entrepreneurs, ten are exporting their products abroad. Out of 10 export women entrepreneurs, seven (70%) export textile products.
- Out of 10 women entrepreneurs exporting goods to foreign countries, seven (70%) of them export their products to two destinations abroad. The women entrepreneurs' exporting to more than two countries are only seven (30%) which denotes that the women entrepreneurs are yet to reach other export destinations.

Suggestion

- Women entrepreneurs should be encouraged to start their enterprise as joint stock companies rather than as sole trade and partnership concerns to avail of the advantages of large scale operation.
- Adequate arrangements have to be made for the supply of credit facility.
- Access to modern machines, skills and training in the area of potential for economically viable projects should be made easy.
- Government should establish market facilities to sell the products and arrange to get finance in time.
- Society needs to change its negative attitude towards women entrepreneurs. Women should be judged based on merits instead of sex.

Conclusion

It is found that being married and having a family is an important source of support. Women entrepreneurs find themselves trying to strike a balance between the role of an organizer of home and a business person. This situation often induces both stress and guilt. For starting, running and development of their business, women need a strong support at home. It needs to be noted that women entrepreneurs were more positive about the effects of the business on their quality of life. However, lack of time is the main difficulty faced by these entrepreneurs. It is reflected from of our social norms that running home and looking after family is the primary responsibility of women.

The primary qualities that make a person a successful entrepreneur have nothing to do with the difference in sex. Though the combination of factors depends on personal and individual priorities, certain essential ingredients are a must for outstanding success in the fields. They are initiative, creative ability, never-say-die spirit, the resilient power to transform crushing setbacks to dazzling challenges, wide-ranging networking and pragmatism. It should be possible for one to develop a nurtured idea into a good business, model. There is nothing like the zeal and zest to learn from others' success. Aspiring entrepreneurs can hope to benefit from a close study of the methods of veteran entrepreneurs. One brilliant idea can keep you going, and the difference in gender is of no consequence. A person need not be gifted with any magical powers to convert a fond dream into a path-breaking reality. What is required is a sense of proportion in the endeavor and the determination to strengthen the sagging morale whenever necessary. The bottom line is that growth depends on our capacity and the sky is the limit.

If this dissertation is any way motivates the struggling women entrepreneur the purpose of this study would have been apply rewarded.

Bibliography

Agrawal, Meenu Women *Empowerment and Globalization*, Kanishka Publictions.

Balram Dogra and kharminder Ghuman, *Rural Marketing: Concepts and Practices*, Tata McGraw-Hill Publications.

Beena, C. and Sushma B, "Women Entrepreneurs Managing petty business-A study from motivational perspectives", Southern Economics, Vol. 42, No. 2, pp. 5-8, May 15, 2003.

Bhatnagar, Naresh, "potters wheel Development—A Necessity for rual growth", *Journal of Rural Technology*, vol. 2, p. 46.

Dhameja, S.K., *Women Entrepreneurs*, Deep and Deep Publications.

Ganesan. S, *Status of Women Entrepreneurs in India*, Kanishka Publictions.

Gupta, C.B and Dr. Srinivasan, N.P., *Entrepreneurship Development in India*, Sultan Chand & Sons.

Gupta, K.C., *Progress and Prospects of Pottery Industry in India*, Mittal Publications.

Guptha, Charu Smith, "Clay-traditional material for making Handicrafts", *Indian Journal of Traditional Knowledge*, vol. 7, p. 116-124.

Hooda, *Statistics for Business and Economics*, McMillan Publications.

Jeet, Sumati, *Handicraft year book 1986*, Handicraft Industry, p. 413.

Kamalakannan, K. (2005) Journal of Kurukshetra, April 2005, pp. 10-13.

Kasthuri, V. Manickavasagam and Jayanthi P "Women Entre-preneurs: An Analysis. Southern Economist 2007, May 1.

Kothari, C.R., Research Methodology—Methods and techniques, second Edition (2004), *Wiswaprakashan*, p. 2-5, p. 31-33, p. 55 57, p. 233-236, p. 256-258.

Kothari, C.R., *Research Methodoloy*, Methods and techniques, second Edition (2004), *Wiswaprakashan*, p. 2-5, p. 31-33, p. 55-57, p. 233-236, p. 256-258.

Kumar, A. Selva, *Plight of Unorganised Sector*, Discovery Publishing House Pvt. Ltd., New Delhi.

Mathu, UC, *Rural Marketing Text and Cases*, Excel Publishing.

Mukherjee, Sujata (2006) "What motivate women entrepreneurs-Factor influencing their motivation". The ICFAI Journal of Entrepreneurship Development, 3(4) Dec., pp. 7-20.

Naraisaiah M. Lakshmi and P. Sreenivasanaidu *Artisan Industry and Rural Development*, Discovery Publishing House, New Delhi, 2006.

North Western India Study-Social Welfare, July-Aug 2008.

Parathasarathy, "Tradition and Change: Artisan Producers in Gujarat, *Journal of entrepreneurship*, vol. 8, No. 1, p. 45.

R. Vasanthagopal & Dr. Santha, *Women Entrepreneurs in India*, New Century Publications.

Richard. Levin, *Statistics for Management*, Tata McGraw-Hill Publications.

Sujatha.V, Gomathi, V. Savithri, V. and Parveen Banu, M.A. Entrepreneurial Development, Kaveri Publication.

Virze, Medha Dulhashi, *Women Entrepreneurs in India*, Mittal Publications.

Index

S